Organization Development Annual
Volume IV

Intervening in Client Organizations

Conrad N. Jackson
and Michael R. Manning
Editors

ASTD

AMERICAN SOCIETY
FOR TRAINING AND
DEVELOPMENT

1640 KING STREET
BOX 1443
ALEXANDRIA, VIRGINIA
22313-2043

Published by:

AMERICAN SOCIETY FOR TRAINING AND DEVELOPMENT

1640 KING STREET
BOX 1443
ALEXANDRIA, VIRGINIA
22313-2043
703/683-8100

Contents

Foreword 1

PART ONE: The Intervention Step in the Consulting Task
  1. Anatomy of an OD Intervention
      Conrad N. Jackson and Michael R. Manning.....................5
  2. Team Building: Suggestions for Redirection
      Donald D. Bowen 16
  3. Family Business Consulting: Facilitating Business Transition in
      Closely Held Companies
      Nancy A. Oretskin, Stephen L. McClure, and
      Michael R. Manning..25

PART TWO: Important Contributions to OD Theory and Practice
  4. Intervention Theory and Method
      Chris Argyris 47
  5. Choosing the Depth of Organizational Intervention
      Roger Harrison 53
  6. Strategic Pay and High-Involvement Organizations: Interview
      With Edward Lawler
      Conrad N. Jackson...69

PART THREE: Examples of Interventions in Industry
  7. Socio-Technical Redesign of an HR Division
      Joseph S. Fiorelli and Mark Kizilos 91
  8. Ethnographic Work Modeling Interventions
      Larry D. Loehr..106
  9. Implementing Self-Managed Teams in a Company's Most
      Productive and Profitable Plant: Why Risk Change?
      Patricia V. Averett..122
  10. Esso's New Directions: Review of a Major Organisational
      Effectiveness Intervention
      Clyde McMillan 136

PART FOUR: Emerging Issues in OD
  11. Insights on International Management and Organization
      Development: Interview With Nancy Adler
      Beverly A. Battaglia 155
  12. TQM: OD's Role in Implementing Value-Based Strategies
      Melville Adams 168

Foreword

Intervention is the phase of organization development (OD) consultation toward which everything else points. However a relatively small percentage of clients with whom we faced entry issues will actually get this far. It seems that new forms of (and indeed rationales about) intervention are being devised almost constantly. Many of these are never widely reported, so it is not easy to keep up with what is going on or judge which of these events are likely to prove significant. In this volume, however, we will try to reexamine some important familiar interventions, describe some recent developments, and consider some important principles which help explain why we do what we do.

In Chapter 1, we suggest that individual motivation can be viewed as a sort of common denominator for all interventions, and suggest some ways to use it as a lens through which to evaluate the potential of intervention activities. Donald Bowen then dissects one of the old standard OD interventions—team building—in Chapter 2, arguing that self-disclosure is the key to its success. He suggests some re-targeting of team building applications. Nancy Oretskin, Stephen McClure, and Michael Manning (Chapter 3) follow with some principles for intervening in closely held companies, including some suggestions for diagnosing family dynamics.

In the second section of the book, we look back on some key conceptual contributions which have helped shape the OD field. A section of Chris Argyris's *Intervention Theory and Methods* is reprinted in Chapter 4, presenting the three key intervention tasks of generating valid data, encouraging free and informed choice, and building internal commitment. Roger Harrison's classic piece, "Choosing the Depth of an Organizational Intervention," follows in Chapter 5 and suggests that OD consultants should not force an intervention's level deeper than the client's energy and resources are inclined to take it. In Chapter 6, Ed Lawler reflects on some of the key learnings of his distinguished career, and discusses his approach to consultation. He also updates some of his recent thinking about performance-based pay and high-involvement management.

Section three of this volume provides four examples of different kinds of interventions in actual use. Joseph Fiorelli and Mark Kizilos (Chapter 7) begin with a description of a socio-technical redesign in a large division of a global firm. Larry Loehr (Chapter 8) follows with a description of an ethnographic work modeling intervention in a large utility. Patricia Averett (Chapter 9) then discusses her experiences in implementing self-managed work teams in an already successful plant of a Fortune 200 company. Finally, in Chapter 10, Clyde McMillan describes a multi-faceted, long-term, and large-scale intervention undertaken by a major oil company in Australia.

In the final section of this volume, we present viewpoints on two emerging organizational issues that must be addressed by OD practitioners. In Chapter 11, Beverly Battaglia's interview with Nancy Adler explores cross-cultural issues faced by organizations when they become international. Finally, Melville Adams offers a critique of traditional OD practices in light of a second wave of scientific management in the form of total quality management (TQM).

As usual, many thanks are in order to those who helped facilitate this volume; some of whom we acknowledge here. We would like to start with our employers, the University of Alabama in Huntsville and New Mexico State University, for providing us with many kinds of support for our various editing and writing tasks. ASTD also has been helpful in many ways, including Beverly Battaglia's consistently helpful encouragement and support on behalf of the OD Professional Practice Area and Joanne Puerling's shepherding of the manuscripts into a finished volume. Last, and certainly not least, special thanks to our spouses, Suzanne and Nancy, for their support and companionship during what has turned out to be (for many reasons) a rather adventuresome year in our lives.

Conrad N. Jackson, Ph.D.
and Michael R. Manning, Ph.D.
Editors, ASTD Organization Development Annual Series

Part One: The Intervention Step in the Consulting Task

1. Anatomy of an OD Intervention

Conrad N. Jackson and Michael R. Manning

> Organizations don't change [and] groups don't change, unless their individual members change. How can the OD consultant foster the changes in individuals which result in the change of the entire client system?

Intervention is the step in the OD consultation process where plans and hopes and fears are put to the ultimate test. No matter how well consultants can sell their services, and no matter how pure their motives and insightful their diagnoses, unless interventions are well-conceived, skillfully facilitated, and carried out with client commitment, the intended changes in the client system will not be likely to occur.

Guiding behavioral changes in groups of people remains an uncertain art. Many types of interventions may seem relevant to any given situation. Consultants develop their own frames of reference for understanding the client systems they observe, and their own set of favorite tools for intervening in these systems. However, there are times when we face perplexing organizational situations and can use some fresh insights into the causes and ways to impact them.

This chapter describes a framework that we find helpful when selecting and designing interventions. We believe that using this framework facilitates the production of desirable organizational changes, while helping to minimize undesirable impacts. We hope other consultants and their clients might also find this framework useful.

The Function of an Intervention

An intervention is an activity which comes between a preexisting state and a resulting state. OD interventions are (usually) planned events which break the normal transition from dysfunctional human processes to the undesirable outcomes they cause, facilitating instead a transition to a desired outcome. (See Figure 1 on the following page.)

Some social interventions put most of their emphasis on the first of these tasks–interrupting the normal dysfunctional transition. For example, apprehending criminals and confining them in prisons can discourage them from committing more crimes when they return to the outside world. Likewise, using Robert's Rules of Order in a meeting helps a majority limit discussion of an issue with which a minority is uncomfortable.

Other interventions emphasize the second of the tasks outlined in Figure 1–facilitation of the desired processes. Weight loss programs, for

---

Conrad Jackson, Ph.D., is Associate Professor of Management at the University of Alabama in Huntsville, Huntsville, AL 35899. Michael Manning, Ph.D., is Associate Professor of Management at New Mexico State University, Las Cruces, NM 88003.

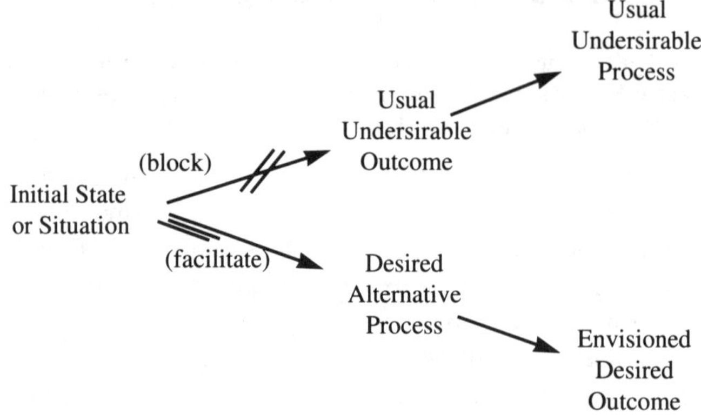

example, verbally encourage people to direct their hunger toward maintaining or forming good eating habits such as eating appropriate foods in appropriate amounts. Similarly, training programs provide positive role models and verbal encouragement. OD interventions generally combine both the blocking of dysfunctional processes that have been identified by diagnosis and the encouragement of desirable alternative processes. For example, the consultant might say to a meeting participant, "Mary, I can see you have some energy for discussing Bill's supervisory style, but for now let's continue prioritizing these issues to reach consensus on which one we will tackle first."

Breaking Old Routines

Many interventions become widely used because alternatives have been found to be ineffective or infeasible. On a societal level, for example, exhorting criminals to "Just Say No!" is not a favored approach to deterring drug addicts from stealing and fencing car stereos to get money to buy drugs. Even teaching them job skills would not likely deter their criminal activity if they live in a cultural milieu where holding a job is considered a stupid thing to do.

In this case, a strong outside force such as apprehension and incarceration is usually considered necessary to deter this sort of criminal activity. But this intervention works on only one side of the change problem (i.e., it temporarily forestalls the criminal's ability to perpetrate crimes against the general public). It does little to blunt the desire for drugs or increase appreciation for active employment.

"Making an example" of employees who are frequently tardy by suspending them without pay is also a one-sided intervention. It may cause them to try to avoid being caught, but it doesn't necessarily make them want to be at work on time.

Some interventions are impoverished in the opposite way. For example, society does not give weight loss organizations authority to come into one's house, put his refrigerator under lock and key, and parcel out food only in a healthy and appropriate manner. Likewise, a trainer is not empowered to follow trainees back into the workplace and fill out performance appraisals based on how they use their new skills.

The emphasis in these interventions must be on demonstrating and exhorting the use of a better way to manage one's life or work. And just as it is widely reported that most dieters put weight back on within two years or less, the subjects of many other "show them a better way" interventions tend to slide back into old familiar behaviors. These examples illustrate the maxim that people tend to resist change. Deep psychological, cultural, and political ruts bind us to familiar (and often not totally desirable) behavior patterns.

Complex Human Systems and Resistance to Change

Clearly the challenges facing OD consultants are great. If getting individuals to change is complicated and difficult, getting groups and systems to change can be even more so. Groups are affected by norms and roles that guide and constrain them, as well as by the multiple and sometimes conflicting motives of their individual members.

Successful OD consultants must block the behaviors that result from dysfunctional norms, so they can begin to teach and facilitate productive new norms. For example, members of a group may habitually advocate specific solutions in a discussion even before there has been a consensual definition of the problem. In this case, the consultant must focus the discussion on problem definition, while interrupting and deflecting any attempts to advocate or evaluate solutions.

It has been said that human systems in an organization are somewhat like an iceberg: The most important elements are hidden beneath the surface. Thus, a consultant is rightfully concerned with what people are thinking and feeling and wanting, in addition to what actually can be seen (i.e., what they are actually doing). But it adds significantly to the complexity of the consultant's task if we expect him or her to change what people think (much less feel or want).

Values and attitudes are particularly resistant to change. So it is important to focus on behavior change as the fundamental goal. Clients generally understand why this is important. For example, one worker might say to another, "I don't really care if you like me or not, but I do care whether you treat me with respect." The bottom line is that no matter what a person thinks about a situation, it is his or her behavior—giving you advanced notice that an issue will be discussed during an upcoming meeting, voting for a proposal, openly confronting someone with his or her concerns — that really matters.

The primacy of behaviors is not advocated simply because we are unable to assure the validity of our assumptions about what others are thinking or feeling. It also stems from the observation that when people try a new behavior, they often find that they like it. In fact, we are more likely to see an attitude change as a result of a change in behavior than we are to see the opposite.

This is a part of the logic of using quotas in EEO programs: Eliminate discriminatory behaviors, and discriminatory attitudes will begin to disappear. Thus, in designing interventions, the consultant must devote sufficient attention to identifying and addressing desirable and undesirable behaviors. This includes encouraging a degree of openness to trying a new behavior.

The Group as the Sum of Individuals

In the presence of the group, individuals begin to respond to norms which they do not necessarily follow outside of the group context. For example, several committee members may carry on various conversations with each other just prior to the start of a meeting. Once the meeting starts, the group norms of "one conversation at a time" and "don't interrupt the person who holds the floor" begin to operate strongly. This is one reason why many OD consultants view a group as much more than just the sum of the individuals.

In a literal sense, however, a group or organization only changes when the relevant behaviors of its individual members change. To that extent, then, the group is precisely the sum of its individual members. Further, the "behavior of the group" can be changed only by changing the behavior of its members. Thus, while we infer a norm of not interrupting the speaker, what actually occurs is that each individual member of the group believes that this behavior is the appropriate and accepted thing that he or she must do.

When we set out to change a group, we expect some people to change more quickly, readily, and effectively than others. In marketing terms, there may be pioneers, early adopters, etc. (cf, Rodgers, 1983). Therefore, we must first bring about change in these early adopters. When enough of the members (particularly the group's informal and formal leaders) make a change, the norms of the group are likely to change. Aligning this powerful force in the desired direction fosters change toward congruence by more of the later adopters.

Types of Individual Motives

We can, therefore, benefit from understanding a change process through the motivational lens of the individual members. By influencing individual group members to change, we can leverage the adoption of new norms by others. But we must recognize norms as only one of many motivational forces acting on individuals which must be considered by the OD consultant.

Every individual is bombarded with thousands of potential and often conflicting behavioral choices each day, though relatively few are actually acted upon. These choices may be as seemingly mundane as saying "hello" to the guy in the next office, as politically complicated as telling a co-worker you think she is wrong about an opinion she expressed, as unconsciously risky as leaving one's phone unattended for a few minutes to get a cup of coffee, as consciously risky as asking the boss for permission to attend an executive meeting, as primal as muttering rude remarks about the driver who took your parking place, or as culturally mandated as putting on a tie for work.

Some issues may continue to confront us moment to moment during much of the day. Such issues often remain at a partially or fully unconscious level, though the underlying drive may be simple enough. For example, one may feel occasional hunger pangs long before consciously considering whether it is time to go to lunch. Or, though it may provoke anger, one might never consciously consider confronting a person who made an offensive remark in a meeting. Figure 2 depicts four categories of motivational forces which could be acting on every one of an individual's behavioral decisions.

Figure 2: Four Categories of Motivational Forces

Individuals' Awareness of Their Motives

		Conscious	Unconscious
	From Within Self	Goals, Intentions	Personality, Drives, and Habits
Initiating Source of the Motive			
	From Within Another	Contracts, Rules, and Models	Culture and Normative Forces

We don't have the time or emotional energy to go through a complicated weighing of the motivational forces resulting from each item. Therefore, we revert to habits and norms that provide us with simple and/or automatic choices. These are the familiar ruts which guide our life while we husband our limited conscious attention capacity. These ruts allow us to avoid committing the time and energy necessary to undergo a conscious rational decision process unless the issue is considered especially salient (i.e., an important or attractive opportunity, or a consequential threat). For example, even though I am uncomfortable wearing a tie, once I have bothered to put one on, I usually wear it all day. While at work, the issue of removing it usually fails to pass beyond some threshold of importance, so it receives no conscious consideration.

Mobilizing Motivational Forces for Change

The consultant's job may be viewed as getting the client group members to direct their behaviors in prescribed ways, instead of being guided by the ease and predictability of old patterns and norms. To decide how to apply his or her tools, the change agent must examine the field of motivational forces that act on individual members to determine which of these supports the unproductive behaviors observed, and calculate which ones might restrain or encourage the desired behaviors. Some of the common change and resistance motives that constantly influence an individual's motivation are considered in the following.

■ Goal Direction. Consultants generally prefer the client to be driven by conscious goals. They encourage them to consciously pick goals and identify desired patterns of behavior, especially "owning" decisions. Typical interventions which emphasize the personal goal motive include goal setting (Locke, 1978), the installation of gainsharing or other compensation plans (Lawler, 1986), or strategic planning and the development of vision and mission statements (Weisbord, 1987). Note, however, as might be predicted by Expectancy Theory (Vroom, 1964), that individuals will be motivated by the outcomes they value and by what they believe about the probability of successful achievement of those outcomes — not by what the consultant believes about these things.

■ Contracts and Rules. This set of forces is illuminated by Exchange Theory (Emerson, 1972): People give compliance because they expect to get a valued payoff in return. Thus, one may emit a behavior not because it is intrinsically important, but because it is instrumental in gaining a valued reward. In addition, social learning theory (Bandura, 1977) suggests looking for role models to minimize the possibility of being rejected for breaking some important norm. Role negotiation (Harrison, 1971), planned renegotiation (Sherwood and Glidewell, 1973), new employee orientation, realistic job previews, and job design (Hackman and Oldham, 1980) are interventions that can target this set of motivational forces.

■ Cultural or Normative. These are expectations from our environment with which we comply more or less unconsciously. Prevailing norms do not always promote productivity or satisfaction, however. It is helpful to make people consciously aware of norms so they can be examined, questioned and, if necessary, modified. This is the turf on which traditional OD won its role in contemporary management practice.

Typical interventions may include team building (Dyer, 1987) or process consultation (Schein, 1987).

■ Personality, Drives, and Habits. These are examples of the great variety of forces from our unconscious that constantly impel or shape our actions. One must usually become aware of these inner forces to find ways to minimize their impact. Interventions aimed at these forces might include relapse prevention (Marx, 1982), self discovery exercises, personality assessment, feedback (Lewicki et al., 1988), or videotaping and observing one's own behaviors.

Selecting an Intervention

Consultants often find themselves caught up in a swirl of forces and energies within the client organization. But consulting is not like driving a power boat; simply pointing the bow where you want to go and gunning the engine. The OD consultant's job is more like that of the sailboat skipper. One cannot change the wind, the waves, and the tide. However, one can skillfully apply the technology of the boat, using the surrounding forces of nature to get to the destination.

OD consultants learn they generally cannot (and should not) force change (see Argyris, 1973, reprinted in part in Chapter 4 of this volume). However, it may be necessary to make only a small change in an individual's overall balance of motivational forces to bring about a significant change in his behavior. Consider an angry crowd of people gathered in political protest, emotionally charged, and full of energy. The leaders of the protest may incite the crowd's anger and frustration, and they may even want it to seem a dangerous force. Yet at the same time, the leaders may be worried that some unanticipated action might spark a violent confrontation in which they will be destroyed. This is the notion of the straw that breaks the camel's back.

Consultants try to find some action levers. They wish to leverage individuals' motivations toward the desired change and avoid the pitfalls which arouse resistance. Note that desirable behavior changes can even include tentative and inept efforts, because these starting points can be reinforced and shaped by the facilitator and other members toward the ultimate aims. Thus, consultants must select which of the forces acting on client members they will try to affect, and what strategies they will employ to modify (increase or decrease) them.

Harrison (1970, reprinted in Chapter 5 of this volume) notes that interventions can be classified along a scale from Instrumentality to Intrapersonal Analysis, and recommends that consultants intervene at the least psychological depth that will get the job done. In general, they usually choose to intervene with the least intrusive psychological force (or assistance)—and commitment of time and capital—possible to minimize cost and undesirable side effects. For example, attending a training seminar would be unnecessary if a brief piece of feedback would achieve the same thing. Similarly, undergoing a full-scale socio-technical intervention would be unnecessary if a simple team building exercise would suffice.

On the other hand, there is little sense (and much danger) in using an intervention that is not likely to be enough to have an effect. One risks wasting valuable time and money. This not only makes the client system weaker, but also may reinforce the belief that "things will just never change around here," which often becomes a self-fulfilling prophecy.

The type and intensity of intervention used in any given situation is, of course, ultimately the consultant's and client's judgment call. No complete and unerring model or plan for making such a selection exists. But consultants must try to avoid the Law of the Hammer ("Give a child a hammer, and he will discover that everything needs to be beaten.") which can lead to peddling one's favorite cures regardless of the client's real needs. Therefore, to select an appropriate intervention, the consultant should:

■ Examine the types of forces encouraging and restraining individuals (particularly those likely to be on the leading side of the adoption curve) from making a change. What are the needs and issues which they respond to? The four categories of motivational forces mentioned earlier can assist in making this diagnosis.

■ Estimate the likely change gradient (the likelihood that change will result, given the costs of the effort) for each of the four types of motivational forces, and the likelihood that a sufficient amount of change will be generated by each to bring about a fair trial of the innovation. Consider the impacts on individuals' goals; and not on just the "official" ones considered desirable.

■ Select the least costly method likely to get the job done. For example, clients may be concerned that they have too few qualified people ready for promotion to new positions in their rapidly growing company. An examination of the situation may show that managers do little to train their people for supervisory responsibilities. The problem may be that managers don't know how to mentor and develop people, or that they have little time to do so. Or perhaps, somewhat more insidiously, some managers may hate to have good employees promoted just as they seem to be learning the job. Further, recognize that these supervisors have a lot on their agendas besides employee development.

The consultant, after assessing this situation, may consider several possible interventions.

■ Redesign managers' jobs so fewer expectations are placed on them, and so they have more time to attend to employee development.

■ Change the organization's culture to stress the role of supervisors as developers of people—human resources which must be called upon to get things done. Perhaps supervisors' jobs could be changed to "Coach" or "Employee Developer," and they could wear a badge of honor on their collar which corresponds to the number of employees they have had promoted.

■ Alternatively, the organization could have managers attend training sessions where they are videotaped, so they can watch themselves role play development situations in order to look for cues (e.g., body language, feedback skills, etc.) which might discourage employees from taking initiative on projects or developing skills which could help them get promoted.

■ The performance appraisal and compensation systems of the company might be modified to place the same emphasis on employee development as on other measures of departmental productivity.

The consultant may see potential for contributing to the development of more promotable talent in any or all of the above, but may expect that the largest impact will occur only if the managers themselves target the outcome. Thus, consultants would seek to use an intervention that encourages managers to own this goal or that ties this objective to another goal the client already values. The last alternative may prove to be the least complicated and least costly way of achieving this.

Conscious Level is Critical

While wise consultants usually attempt to align a number of motives from most or all of the four sectors in the direction of the desired behaviors, the fundamental role of consultants is to help the client identify and raise key choices to the conscious level. They help clients define the issues that require their attention, and unmask the unconscious motives of personality and habit that can lead them astray. They can also help individuals to embrace the subtle parts of their unconscious that may be extremely functional. And finally, they encourage goals, norms, and contracts that reinforce effectiveness.

Summary and Conclusions

The field of OD has experienced much change over the past decades. Important roots of OD, such as T-groups, are used little today. Many of the interventions which followed, such as team building are being de-emphasized now in favor of large-scale macro techniques. The consultant is sometimes caught in a bind, trying to decide how to pack enough punch into an intervention to expedite change, while minimizing cost, emotional casualties, letdown, and backlash. Traditional theory suggests that the consultant should generally look for the minimum force which can be shifted to get key behaviors to change. The goal is to tap a sufficient motive without wasting time, money, and emotional energy on overkill. One way to do this is to understand how our interventions impact the individuals they must change.

The motives affecting an individual at any one time include conscious goals, contracts, unconscious norms, and unconscious individual motives such as personality and habits. If consultants can determine the most potent forces influencing individuals involved in an intervention, and knows which of these can be impacted (encouraged or blocked)— especially within the opinion leaders — they have an idea where to best direct an intervention. As Lewin (1951) pointed out during the emergence of OD as a discipline, consultants are always intervening in a force field, and never in a situation which has one simple issue or cause. Thus, in the end, sensitivity is an essential part of both the consultant's method and his or her message.

Some may find it overly ambitious—if not foolishly redundant—to try to view change on the individual level, when some of the most exciting trends in OD seem to be happening at the macro end of the intervention spectrum. For example, the impressive work of Merrelyn Emery (1982) in changing whole systems via the technique she calls a "search conference" seems to offer an amazing potential for impacting organizations. By focusing groups of 100 or more people at a time on creating a collective unconscious, members form a common ground upon which interdependent organizational members can pursue the strategic future they desire.

No doubt many other innovative and powerful methods will be introduced in the coming years, perhaps yielding successful changes that are scarcely imagined today. Yet, we believe that examining the motivational forces acting on the individuals within a group (such as Emery's focus on the collective unconscious) may help suggest further innovative ways to affect these forces at the collective level (such as her search conferences).

We would not, of course, reject the use of a reliably effective intervention just because we didn't know exactly how it caused change to occur on the individual level. However, we believe the quest to understand more about what makes individuals change can result in greater knowledge about how to change organizations and groups.

References

Argyris, Chris. *Intervention Theory and Method: A Behavioral Science View.* Reading, Massachusetts: Addison-Wesley, 1973.

Bandura, Albert. *Social Learning Theory.* Englewood Cliffs, New Jersey: Prentice-Hall, 1977.

Dyer, William G. *Team Building: Issues and Alternatives.* 2d ed. Reading: Addison-Wesley, 1987.

Emerson, Richard M. "Exchange Theory (Parts I and II)," In J. Berger, M. Zelditch, and B. Anderson. (eds.) *Sociological Theories in Progress, Vol. II,* Boston: Houghton Mifflin, 1972.

Emery, Merrelyn. *Times Searching: For New Directions in New Ways for New Times.* Canberra: Centre for Continuing Education, Australian National University, 1982.

Hackman, J.R. and Oldham, Gregg R. *Work Redesign.* Reading, Massachusetts: Addison-Wesley, 1980.

Harrison, Roger. "Role Negotiations." In W. Burke and H. Hornstein (eds.) *The Social Technology of Organization Development.* Washington, D.C.: NTL Learning Resources, 1971.

Harrison, Roger. "Choosing the Depth of Organizational Intervention." *The Journal of Applied Behavioral Science,* 6 no. 2, (1970): pp. 182–202.

Lawler, Edward E., III. *High Involvement Management.* San Francisco: Jossey-Bass, 1986.

Lewicki, Roy J., Bowen, Donald D., Hall, Douglas T., and Hall, Francine S. *Exercises in Management and Organizational Behavior,* 3d ed. New York: John Wiley, 1988.

Lewin, Kurt. *Field Theory in Social Science.* New York: Harper & Row, 1951.

Locke, Edwin A. "The Ubiquity of the Technique of Goal Setting in Theories of and Approaches to Employee Motivation." *Academy of Management Review,* (July 1978): p. 600.

Marx, Robert D. "Relapse Prevention for Managerial Training: A Model for Maintenance of Behavior Change." *Academy of Management Review,* 7 no. 3, (1982): pp. 433-44.

Rogers, Everett M. *Diffusion of Innovations,* 3d ed. New York: McMillan Publishers, 1983.

Schein, Edgar H. *Process Consultation, Vol. II.* Reading, Massachusetts: Addison-Wesley, 1987.

Sherwood, John J. and Glidewell, John C. "Planned Renegotiation—A Norm-Setting OD Intervention." In J. Jones and J. Pfeiffer. (eds.) *The 1973 Annual Handbook for Group Facilitators.* San Diego: University Associates, 1973, pp. 195–202.

Vroom, Victor H. *Work and Motivation.* New York: John Wiley, 1964.

Weisbord, Marvin R. *Productive Workplaces.* San Francisco: Jossey-Bass, 1987.

2. Team Building: Suggestions for Redirection

Donald D. Bowen

French and Bell (1990) proclaim team building interventions to be "probably the most important single group of interventions in OD..." (p. 127). Current team building practice seems to be preoccupied with fixing existing teams that have gone astray. However, the major benefit to be gained from team building might be applying it to new teams to help them avoid problems and to give them a head start on their tasks. Given the truly impressive advantage that a cohesive team acquires in motivating team members toward team goals, I believe that we should try to enhance teamwork from the start. In this chapter we will consider how to exploit some clear lessons from social psychology about creating cohesiveness in teams in order to raise the levels of productivity and quality in organizations.

Focus on Task Relationships

The primary objective of team building as described in most organization development literature is to promote the effectiveness of the team in task performance through provision of task structure in the form of specific goals, priorities, procedures, role definitions, etc. Creation of effective, satisfying, and/or harmonious interpersonal relationships is of concern only to the extent that team relationships are necessary for more effective task performance. Team process issues sometimes become so secondary that they are either ignored or relegated to the status of "what to do if all else fails." Examples abound. Beckhard (1972) prescribes four purposes to team building: setting goals and priorities, analyzing or allocating work, examining group processes, and examining relationships. But Burke (1982, p. 272) admonishes that the four purposes should be pursued in the order listed.

Bell and Rosenzweig (1978) also typify the consensual view when they conclude, "We have come to believe strongly that initial improvement efforts should be task-oriented rather than focused on interpersonal relationships" (p. 392). Fordyce and Weil (1971) suggest that team building activities should seek a balance between attention to tasks and relationships, but the team building design they provide seems heavily task-centered in that it calls for the group to produce "a future action list, with assignments and schedules" (p. 121).

Perhaps the emphasis reflects our clients' need to justify expenditures from tight budgets, a world where tasks and results are more acceptable than process and relationships.

French and Bell identify four specific varieties of team building activities: task performance, member relationships, group processes, and role relationships. However, they recommend that the consultant should

Donald Bowen, Ph.D., is Professor of Management at The University of Tulsa, Tulsa, OK 74104.

always attempt to implement the client's (rather than the consultant's) goals in a team building intervention. French and Bell do indicate that relationship issues frequently emerge during the process of analyzing the problems the team is experiencing in pursuing its tasks, but they devote the bulk of their discussion to task-centered activities.

To the extent that the OD literature reflects North American culture, it is hardly surprising that the purposes of team building should be envisioned in such hard-nosed, no-nonsense, bottom line terms. The appeal to values of pragmatism, profit, and the Protestant Ethic is self-evident. The instrumentality of team building for accomplishment of serious work is acceptable and legitimate. The notion that human beings might be able to derive greater pleasure and satisfaction from team relationships (the very aspect of team building which is a major psychic reward to those of us who do it) has something of the character of a dirty little secret. What manager in his or her right mind would pay us to perpetrate such "touchy-feely" foolishness?

New Teams or Old Teams?

Perhaps the bias toward a task focus also stems from the fact that almost all of the discussion of team building in present literature assumes that the teams to be developed are on-going teams with a past history of working together that has generated problems for the group (Beckhard, 1972; Burke, 1982; Dyer, 1987; Fordyce & Weil, 1971). Dyer devotes only one of fourteen chapters to new or start-up teams, and even here, his prescription is to deal strictly with task issues. Dyer's chapter on the new team proposes a four-step approach.

■ Develop realistic priority levels in terms of the personal commitments which people bring to the new group. (It is instructive that Dyer does not propose attempting to elevate these commitments, only that members should attempt to understand where each stands.)

■ Share expectations.

■ Clarify goals.

■ Formulate operating guidelines.

If start-up team development is mentioned at all, it is usually only in passing. For example, Fordyce and Weil suggest that new teams will need more time in "getting acquainted" activities. French and Bell recognize that new teams represent an opportunity for team building, but they do not provide much guidance on how new teams might need a somewhat different treatment.

In short, the emphasis in existing OD literature on task-focused team building with existing or on-going teams overlooks some important team building opportunities.

In Figure 1, almost all of the prescriptions would fall into Cell I, with only an occasional suggestion that development of new teams needs to place greater emphasis on Cell IV activities.

Figure 1: Four Applications of Team Building

Primary focus on:

Type of group:	Task	Relationships
Ongoing	I	II
Start-up	III	IV

Evidence Against Preoccupation With Task

Not every theorist stresses the task focus currently in vogue. Argyris (1970) has argued strongly that dealing with the interpersonal issues in a group is necessary before other interventions will be effective; interventions of either the Cell II or Cell IV variety. Weisbord (1985) has also suggested the necessity for the priority of interpersonal issues.

> I have never been in a team building meeting where members did not raise the question of trust and its importance to them, even when they did not initially trust each other. A high level of commitment is built on the foundation of mutual trust. Commitment leads to better work, which results in a better mix of planning and doing.... Inevitably, our feelings about membership, control, and the use of our skills influence our motivation, which in turn determines the quality of our work (p. 29).

In contrast to Dyer's view, Weisbord stresses the motivation of team members as a variable rather than as a given quantity — one which may be influenced by the quality of the relationships among the team members.

The Forgotten Ingredient: Commitment

Weisbord's assertion will be understood by any consultant experienced in team building. Indeed, one of the most important reasons for the formation of teams is to achieve a level of motivation and commitment otherwise unattainable. Anyone who has played a team sport knows the spur to extra effort that the team provides.

Recent research confirms the point. Meyer, Paunonen, Gellatly, Goffin and Jackson (1989) have shown that productivity is higher when employees have "affective commitment" (emotional attachment to, identification with, and involvement in the organization). My colleagues and I (Wolfe,

Bowen, and Roberts, 1989) have described a quasi-experimental study where two days of team building with MBA students playing a complex, semester-long, computer-based management simulation led to a head start over "untreated" teams. For the first half of the term, the profit results for the developed teams ran 190 percent of those shown by the untreated teams. Eventually, the untreated teams became as profitable as the experimental group, but when the semester was over, the total earnings for the treated teams exceeded those of the others by approximately eight percent.

The team building activities the treated teams underwent were designed on the premise that mutual attraction could be increased by encouraging levels of self-disclosure among relative strangers. These results coincide with Shils and Janowitz's (1948) classic illustration of the potency of team motivation found in reports of the German Wehrmacht in World War II. Isolated pockets of German soldiers would fight to the last man, even in later stages of the war when the soldiers were well aware that the war was lost. The tenacity of the German infantryman was due to his loyalty to his "buddies," not to the effectiveness of Nazi propaganda as had been widely believed. Similar findings are available for American troops in both World War II and Korea (Little, 1964).

There appears to be a compelling argument for focusing greater attention on the relationships aspect in team building, particularly with new teams. When cohesion is high, team members will exert themselves for team objectives far beyond what they might normally contribute to achieve their personal goals. The studies of the military indicate that such commitment to the team can achieve levels where individuals literally "lay down their lives" for each other. We know that solidarity or cohesiveness of the primary group does not guarantee effectiveness of the team in terms of the organization's objectives (Seashore, 1954), only those of the team. Managerial leadership will always be necessary to align team and organizational aims. However, if we overlook the potential of cohesiveness to enhance motivation, the full potential of the group to perform its tasks remains barely tapped. The management which succeeds in attaining even a fraction of this level of motivation enjoys a clear competitive edge.

The Key: Self-Disclosure

How do we create cohesiveness? One observer, reviewing the social psychological literature on the development of friendly relationships concludes that:

> Communication, including self-disclosure...is the most important and inclusive attribute of all the attributes of a friendly relationship. It determines the structure and consequences of the relationship (Gupta, 1983, p. 17).

Stokes, Fuehrer and Childs (1983) created experimental groups and demonstrated that groups characterized by high self-disclosure (provided that the level wasn't so high as to create discomfort) perceived themselves to be more cohesive. They also reviewed the literature and concluded that while the relationship is not necessarily simple and linear, it is a fair generalization that self-disclosure tends to create the mutual attraction of cohesiveness.

A manager with Arthur Young (Marksbury, 1979) describes how the team building experience he underwent with other AY managers created a liking and affection for his colleagues through self-disclosure.

> I like them. There is a lot more to them than I originally thought there was. The habitual mask and gestures of self-concealment, playing it safe, 'mindlessly' playing it the way that has worked many times before—they fall away. The others see and are seen. They see me and I see them (pp. 56-57).

It would seem that only by dropping our defenses do we permit others to know us well enough to find something to like and appreciate. Perhaps even more to the point, the quotation also suggests how self-disclosure should enhance another indispensable ingredient of effective teams — mutual trust.

Archer and Earle (1983; Archer 1987), in a major review of the social psychological literature, suggest that self-disclosure helps to generate two important types of feedback in groups: feedback on our own behavior from which we come to know ourselves, and feedback on how the participants experience the developing relationship. Such feedback helps group members define the nature of the relationship, and "...mutual disclosure may serve as a 'hot line' to explain motives and so prevent unnecessary escalation of conflict" (p. 305). What consultant has not found that many of the conflict issues in organizations arise when managers misinterpret each other?

This process of building teams through self-disclosure, then, is especially relevant when a group of relative strangers must come together and quickly become motivated to contribute extraordinary effort. Many task forces and project teams meet these criteria, especially since they are often formed to deal with crisis situations. But consider the prescriptions we have reviewed from the literature with their emphasis on structuring the group's task and virtual ignoring of the need for group members to come to care for each other.

Team Building Suggestions

Team building with new and start-up teams presents some interesting challenges to the OD profession. Perhaps the greatest challenge is getting clients to recognize the need for start-up team building. It is a rare manager (with a few notable exceptions) who recognizes that establishing a new committee, a new task force, or even a new department should include some intensive team building to assure that the new group is off to a running start. (Most managers, however, will agree that they would not expect a football team to be effective without plenty of pre-game practice — an analogy I have found useful in bringing the need for team building to their attention).

Given that the client sees the need, then what type of intervention is indicated? Rather than attempt to catalog specific team building activities (Gerard Egan, 1971 and 1977, has suggested a number of useful activities which might be used or adapted), I will enumerate some major concerns which the team building consultant must deal with to facilitate the highly cohesive and highly committed teams described here. Roughly, in the following order, the consultant should address the following.

■ Set the tone early. In both the design of the workshop and in his or her opening remarks to participants, the facilitator should urge the development of norms and a climate of openness, mutual respect, and risk-taking. One means of promoting the necessary psychological safety is to hold initial (at least) sessions at an off-site location.

■ Model self-disclosing behavior. A role model will be necessary to help participants develop what may be a new skill for many. One of the ways in which I model what I preach is to tell the participants precisely what I am up to. Moreover, as I introduce activities to promote self-disclosure, I also participate if I possibly can.

■ Help them understand their experiences. Interventions to assist participants in evaluating their experience will also be necessary. Most of them will arrive with a widely held view of how relationships develop. (See the top half of Figure 2.) However, what they will experience looks much more like the bottom half of the figure.

Figure 2: Assumptions About How Relationships Develop

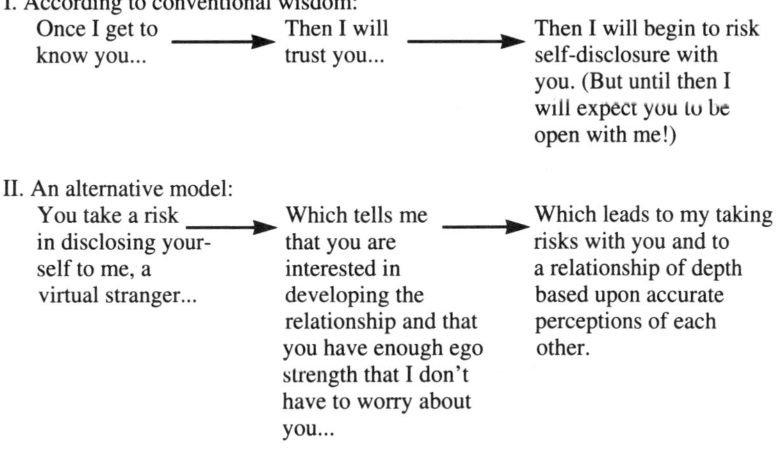

■ Practice, practice, practice. Most participants will need some extensive practice in providing non-evaluative and descriptive feedback. As indicated above, feedback which helps us to understand ourselves and create the relationship is central to the process (see Lewicki et al., 1988, p. 60).

■ Impart group skills. Training in understanding and managing group process is probably also useful to help team members maintain control of how the team functions as it goes about its tasks.

■ Sharpen task understanding. Role definition, goal development, and design of team procedures (as specified in task-centered team building) are also obviously needed. My preference, however, is to hold off introducing these tasks until after the team's interpersonal climate has begun to gel.

■ Reinforce with symbolic experiences. There are certain activities which bear meanings in our culture that are useful in developing highly cohesive teams. Preparing and eating meals together provides many opportunities for participants to take care of one another. Group sports activities are likely to provide shared experiences of adventure and accomplishment as well as important symbolic indications of the group's commitment to operating together as a team. Depending upon climate, facilities, participants' physical condition, and similar considerations, I have found activities ranging from mixed-sex soccer games to such informal activities as throwing a frisbee or hiking through the woods to be important events in the development of the group.

Occasionally the OD consultant will encounter the participant who is either naturally defensive or who finds the situation threatening, and who, thus, cannot enter into a sufficient level of self-disclosure without experiencing debilitating anxiety or damaging his/her career. Managers seem to have a pretty good feel for whether their subordinates could have difficulties in this type of team building and can alert the consultant to the possible problem.

One solution may be to offer the defensive individual a role as a consultant to the team (rather than as a full-fledged member). This arrangement will provide a solution where the team has access to the expert's resources, but where neither the team nor the individual is placed into an unworkable relationship. It seems to me that defensive managers are seldom entrusted with important assignments (except when they possess some technical expertise that makes them absolutely indispensable). Usually the team assignments can be made so that the problem doesn't come up.

Conclusion

Team building with start-up teams may be a better application of the client's time and money than with on-going teams—especially if the tasks facing the group will present an extraordinary challenge and a high

level of commitment. The new team needs interventions which emphasize building relationships as well as solving task problems. To help
client groups achieve extraordinary commitment, I have suggested that
OD consultants need to develop skills in inviting and facilitating self-disclosure in order to telescope the process of promoting cohesiveness in
the group and create a real "do or die" attitude toward the team's objectives. Sociological and social psychological research suggests that such
high performance teams are feasible. It is up to OD professionals to show
how they can become a reality in today's organizations.

References

Archer, R.L. "Commentary: Self-Disclosure, A Very Useful Behavior."
In V. J. Derlega and J.H. Berg (eds.), *Self-Disclosure: Theory, Research,
and Therapy.* New York: Plenum Press, 1987.

Archer, R.L. and Earle, W.B. "The Interpersonal Orientations of
Disclosure." In P.B. Paulus (ed.), *Basic Group Processes.* New York:
Springer-Verlag, 1983.

Argyris, C. *Intervention Theory and Methods, A Behavioral Science View.*
Reading, Massachusetts: Addison-Wesley, 1970.

Beckhard, R. "Optimizing Team-Building Efforts." *Journal of Contemporary Business,* (Summer 1972): pp. 23-37.

Bell, C.H., Jr., and Rosenzweig, J. "Highlights of an Organization
Improvement Program in City Government." In W.K. French, C.H. Bell,
Jr., and R.A. Zawacki (eds.), *Organization Development: Theory, Prac-
tice, Research.* Dallas: Business Publications, Inc., (1978): pp. 380-392.

Burke, W. *Organization Development: Principles and Practices.* Boston:
Little, Brown & Company, 1982.

Dyer, W.G. *Team Building: Issues and Alternatives,* 2d ed. Reading,
Massachusetts: Addison-Wesley, 1978.

Egan, G. *Encounter: Group Processes for Interpersonal Growth.*
Belmont, CA: Wadsworth Publishing Company, 1971.

Egan, G. *You & Me: The Skills of Communicating and Relating to
Others.* Monterey, CA: Brooks/Cole, 1977.

Fordyce, J.K. and Weil, R. *Managing With People: A Manager's Handbook of Organization Development Methods.* Reading, Massachusetts:
Addison-Wesley, 1971.

French, W.L. and Bell, C.H., Jr. *Organization Development,* 4th ed.
Englewood Cliffs, New Jersey: Prentice-Hall, 1990.

Gupta, M. "A Basis for Friendly Dyadic Interpersonal Relationships." *Small Group Behavior,* 14, (1983): pp. 15-33.

Little, R.W. "Buddy Relations and Combat Performance." In M. Janowitz (ed.) *The New Military.* New York: John Wiley, 1964.

Marksbury, H. "A Manager's Trip Through the Hall of Mirrors of the Psyche." *Management Review,* 68 no. 10, (1979): pp. 53-57.

Meyer, J.P., Paunonen, S.V., Gellatly, I.R., Goffin, R.D., and Jackson, D.N. "Organizational Commitment and Job Performance: It's the Nature of the Commitment That Counts." *Journal of Applied Psychology,* 74, (1989): pp. 152-156.

Seashore, S.E. *Group Cohesiveness in the Individual Work Group.* Ann Arbor: University of Michigan, Survey Research References Center, Institute for Social Research, 1954.

Shils, E.A. and Janowitz, M. "Cohesion and Disintegration in the Wehrmacht in World War II." *Public Opinion Quarterly,* 12, (1948): pp. 280-315.

Stokes, J., Fuehrer, A., and Childs, L. "Group Members' Self-Disclosures: Relation to Perceived Cohesion." *Small Group Behavior,* 14, (1983): pp. 63-76.

Weisbord, M.R. "Team Effectiveness Theory." *Training and Development Journal,* 39 no. 1, (1985): pp. 27-29.

Wolfe, J., Bowen, D.D., and Roberts, C.R. "Team Building Effects on Company Performance: A Business Game-Based Study." *Simulation & Games,* 20, (1989): pp. 388-408.

3. Family Business Consulting: Facilitating Business Transition in Closely Held Companies

Nancy A. Oretskin
Stephen L. McClure
Michael R. Manning

Introduction

Family business dynamics titillate everyone's interest. *The Wall Street Journal* frequently launders family feuds and business fortunes with such captivating headlines as "Son Revives Firm by Playing Hardball With Family," "When Family Fires Family, the Ties That Bind End Up Frayed," and "Delights and Dangers of Working for a Family." The television series "Sixty Minutes" once featured the painstaking trials and tribulations of the sale of the Bingham family publishing empire, complete with family versus family confrontations. Even Hollywood depicts the family intertwined in business in its most successful prime time soap operas (e.g., "Dallas," "Dynasty," and "Falcon Crest").

This mystique of family businesses cannot be explained adequately by either business or family dynamics. Rather, it is the power and emotions resulting from the "head-on collision" of both the family and the business that create this captivating intrigue. Consultants who work with family-owned and closely held businesses must be aware of this unique and difficult interaction.

This chapter shares some guidelines and personal insights that we have gained from consulting with family businesses. It discusses the significant and unique steps required in consulting with family businesses, focusing on the key stages of consulting interventions: initial entry, contracting, diagnosis, data collection, and planning.

Since most of our experience with family businesses focuses on the transition of leadership, power, control, and ownership from one generation to the next, this theme will underlie the conceptual basis of this chapter. A common scenario for a consultant's work with family businesses in transition is as follows.

■ The consultant is approached by some member of the family, usually the owner.

■ Conversation between the consultant, the owner, and possibly others in the system produces a contract.

Nancy Oretskin, J.D., is Assistant Professor of General Business and Enterprise at New Mexico State University, Las Cruces, NM, 88003. Steven McClure is a Principal at McClure Consulting, P.O. Box 11011, South Bend, IN 46634. Michael Manning, Ph.D., is Associate Professor of Management at New Mexico State University.

■ Data collection typically involves interviews and observation, but may include other methods.

■ A working session with the owner or owner and relevant family (and future) shareholders ensues (e.g., a two-day retreat).

■ Action plans are produced.

■ Follow-up activities (some involve the consultant usually at critical points) conclude the engagement described in the contract.

Initial Entry

> But Pop it's not 1965 anymore! We need help! You can't continue to make decisions from the seat of your pants. We have invested over a million dollars in state-of-the-art computer equipment and have hired highly-trained personnel. But, nobody knows what they're doing, and there is no direction from you. And if anyone does take some initiative, you're the first one to put them down and stop whatever momentum they have going. I also can't believe you're letting my older brother act as the vice-president of this place. Everyone knows that he doesn't know the business and couldn't manage his way out of a paper bag. Who's gonna run this place? You're not going to be here forever!

> Now you listen to me, Sonny. I started this business before you were a gleam in your mother's eye. I didn't have any computers or high-priced management personnel then, and I did just fine. In fact, I am the guy who turned this business into a multimillion dollar baby, and don't you ever forget it. I still own this place and I'm in charge here until I die—you'll have to carry me out of here. I sent you to college to learn something useful, not to come back and find fault with everything I do around here. What do you think, "The egg" is smarter than "the chicken?"

For the consultant to enter a family business and make a difference, he or she must make initial contact with the founder or the one in the primary power/ownership position: alias, *the chicken. The egg* (the siblings) may very well appreciate the need for intervention by a consultant but lack the requisite power to initiate a successful consulting engagement.

By their very nature, family-controlled organizations often foster greater mistrust of outsiders than public organizations, especially outside consultants who are hired to further one family member's cause against another. The owner—often literally a parent figure to employees—holds the power to hire a consultant, and he or she must be involved no later than the second meeting between the consultant and the client. Also, because the closely held business more clearly reflects the actual identity of the founder or owner than public companies (Schein, 1983), there is a need on the part of founders for a higher degree of trust in the integrity of a consultant.

Very early in the entry stage, consultants should begin to assess the involvement of the various roles played by individuals in the family business system. For instance, what do other family members do? Are there important non-family staff members? Who owns what and how much? Are there some individuals owners who do not work in the business or have any say? How involved are spouses? Is there a board of directors or significant advisor(s), and what is their influence?

Answers to these questions will help the consultant understand early who should be involved in the subsequent phases of consultation. In addition, the owner will likely not see things as others do, so it is important for the consultant to solicit information from more than one source. Nevertheless, as the consulting proceeds, he or she may still need to add others as more is learned about the business and those involved in its operation. For example, it is easy to overlook the spouse at home who may have final input into all business expenditures.

Contracting

Pop! I ran into a guy last night who knows all about family business and transferring the ownership of the business to the kids. I talked to him briefly about our situation; you know whether I should be president or that irresponsible brother of mine. The consultant's coming tomorrow at 10:30. I think you should be there.

Oh, so you think this is the answer, Sonny? Get me in front of an *expert* who agrees with you? I'm sure you don't want your brother there, do you? I suppose you will want this *expert* to test me, so you can get *proof* of how I am not fair to you. Fat chance, Sonny boy!

The two most important issues that need to be resolved in the contracting phase are setting clear expectations and involving the right people.

Setting Clear Expectations

The value and methods of establishing clear expectations for a family business consultation are similar to other OD projects. We have found the work on the "Contracting Meeting" by Block (1988) to be very helpful in setting guidelines that clarify initial expectations of the client and the consultant.

Expectations should be set in two areas: the family and the business. Usually, the owner should expect to work on both family harmony as well as business effectiveness. Many times, the problem for these individuals is the inability to separate family and business issues.

It is with the owner that the family system and the business system often collide. Pressure is exerted from the family to meet legitimate family objectives such as, passing the business on to the child who has been with the business the longest. A counterforce extends from business principles which may, in this case, suggest that the *helm* of the business must be turned over to the most qualified individual, who may not be the child with the greatest tenure. Consequently, the owner is the lightning rod for direct or indirect pressure from both systems.

By assisting the owner in separating family from business sources of pressure early in the relationship, the consultant can provide immediate value by educating the owner, establishing a foundation for future problem solving, and clarifying expectations for the consultation.

Keep in mind that the contract needs to be flexible since it is likely that the intervention will need to change as new information is uncovered (Manning & Locke, 1988). To accomplish this, a certain amount of openness in the contract is necessary. Work between the consultant and selected family members or managers that cannot be anticipated during the contracting phase can often mean the difference between success and failure. For example, in the middle of a recent business succession planning engagement, just prior to a planning retreat, one of the authors arranged for a son to create a document that listed all the areas of agreement between the two generations relative to the transition of ownership of the business. Then a meeting between the father and son was arranged so the document could be discussed, and this document was later circulated to others prior to a planning meeting. (Involved in the ownership transfer were two fathers, who were partners; one father's two sons and the other father's son; plus a non-related manager, who was a peer to all the sons.)

The effect of this unplanned intervention was extremely positive. The parties found that they agreed on a larger number of issues than they originally thought. This allowed the parties to focus on the areas where they differed prior to the meeting. They could also spend much more time during the planning retreat on other issues and details of the transfer where there was not agreement, making the planning meeting much more efficient.

Basic communication regarding who will do what, when, and how must be clearly understood and addressed early in the consultation. This role clarification is the basic foundation for setting clear expectations. The following is an excerpt from a family business strategic planning contracting letter that was sent to a client attempting to clarify his role as consultant.

> My role is that of a catalyst. I will help develop objectives for your family and a strategy looking to the future for Smith Company. I will try to help you institutionalize this process so you can use this structure long after my consulting services are over. I will not be a decision maker, but a tool for the organization to accomplish its goals. Thus, throughout the engagement, I will provide assistance of the following nature:
>
> — I will facilitate Smith family discussion on key and sometimes tough issues. I will also assist individuals and the group in coming to conclusions with the objective of preserving family harmony. This does not mean confrontation will be avoided, but that we will approach confrontation in a manner that is not destructive.
>
> — I will assist the organization in keeping the planning process on track. Once agreement is accomplished, I will play the role of managing the progress toward goal accomplishment. Often, this will mean guiding individuals and groups to keep from becoming bogged down in analyses. A "just sufficient" exploration of factors that contribute to a strategy is an art that is difficult to master by those doing the work.

— It is difficult for individuals within any organization to evaluate themselves without bias. I will provide a review of the key personnel, as well as serve the management team by challenging conclusions. This role will be accomplished from the perspective of an outsider to the organization, but also from my experience with other companies facing the same family/business issues.

— In finding a way for the Smith Company to integrate strategic planning into routine life, I will play the role of change agent. By working with management to experiment with procedures, review their effectiveness, and develop capabilities along the way, I will initially play a very directive role that diminishes over time and is replaced by roles played by members of Smith Company.

Involving the Right People

During initial entry, the consultant should have identified most of the key family and organizational members who should or must be involved in the consultation for its success. The contracting phase clarifies these individuals' identities and expressly communicates this information to all the parties.

To help clarify who must be involved in a family business consultation that emphasizes a transition plan, begin by determining where control in the organization currently lies. Try to identify individuals who either presently influence the direction of the company, have ownership in the company, or play key roles in the day-to-day operation of the business. In addition, it is very important to know the family structure, the number of generations, the children and spouses, and the general capabilities and influence (e.g., stock ownership and/or planned ownership) of all these individuals. Knowing where control lies and the character of the family structure helps define who to involve and at what extent.

For example, a family member who has ownership in the company business but has no responsibility (and no interest) for company operations should be involved in the transition planning, but to a lesser degree than the family member who has ownership and great responsibility in company operations. The former will be involved in deciding issues of transition, ownership, and who runs the business; whereas the latter individual will be involved in all of these decisions, in addition to work that is required in implementing these decisions.

Also, it may be important to ascertain the founder's advisors (banker, accountant, insurance agent, lawyer, etc.), so they may be included in some aspects of future planning. Their insight and understanding of the family can help to develop and implement a more successful transition. The consultant needs to assure these trusted advisors that their work with the client will not jeopardize the relationships they have with the founder. This may be critical in heading off any potential problems down the road. If the owner hears two different things from the consultant and his or her advisors, then the client does nothing.

During the contract phase, a recurring question often arises: "Who is the client?" We believe very strongly that the family shareholders and potential family shareholders are the clients to which consultants have ultimate accountability. The client is not one individual or a small group of shareholders. The significance of this distinction is that the interests of the family shareholders as a group will govern project goals and/or potential conflicts and not the interests of an individual. However, we explain that all family shareholders as well as selected company employees will likely be involved in the process.

Of course, consulting fees and other associated costs should be identified and included in the original contract. This will allow parties to more accurately budget their time and understand the applicable expenses.

Diagnosis

> Hey, Pop, why don't we make joint decisions around here? After all, we'll supposedly be running this place this time next year. Don't you think we have any good ideas?

> Sonny, did you order that last shipment of olive oil? Boy, did you screw up! If I want something done right, I have to do it myself.

After dealing with issues of initial entry and contracting, the family business consultant must begin formalizing his or her diagnosis of the family and business systems. However, we would like to suggest one caveat before proceeding in this linear fashion. Diagnosis after initial entry and contracting is too late. McClure (1990) suggests that diagnosis should be provided at the earliest stage possible in a consulting relationship. This is especially true when working with mid-sized clients that include many family members. For them to determine the value of an OD consultation, they need to know at the very beginning what the consultant will do. Thus, the consultant must quickly assess a situation to help the client see what he or she proposes will, in fact, be of value to the company and, thus, to that family member's interests. Diagnosis is not a distinct stage in a linear process of consulting, but is more accurately a continuing process throughout the life of the consultation. However, it is after initial entry and contracting that consultants experience a crucial need to explicitly clarify the diagnosis of the client organization and then proceed with more data collection.

In family businesses, it is crucial to diagnose not only the business, but also the family system and how both the family and business systems interrelate.

Diagnosing the Business System

Many guidelines exist to aid consultants in the diagnosis of a business system. We find the "Six-Box Model" developed by Weisbord (1990) and the "Diagnostic Selling Model" developed by McClure (1990) to be particularly useful guidelines. Since these models are easily accessible elsewhere, we will not elaborate on them here.

Diagnosing the Family System

Few, if any, models exist that are helpful in the diagnosis of a family system to guide a family business consultation. Therefore, we have developed a simple conceptual scheme that allows us to assess the family system involved in a business. This model emphasizes the importance of how a family manages the making of decisions, and how it deals with differences and conflict.

■ Decisions. Families, like other group decision makers, can make business decisions in a number of ways (Schein, 1988). In many family businesses, decisions are made by one individual, typically the founder/owner. This establishes the power structure in which working family members (as well as other employees) must exist. In other firms, key decisions may be made by a minority coalition of individuals (e.g., the founder/owner and his/her eldest sibling) to the exclusion of others (e.g., founder/owner's spouse, younger siblings, key non-family employees). This type of decision process creates bad feelings with the excluded members and often results in their feeling "railroaded." Still other firms may operate with decisions commonly made by a majority of family/non-family members. Both minority- and majority-rule decision making can cause problems since they involve components of win-lose dynamics to the extent that some individuals' positions are heard and supported, and other individuals' positions are not.

Two more possible ways families can make decisions are by consensus and unanimity. Both of these procedures involve processes where all relevant members are heard and allowed to influence the decision that is made. In the consensus approach, all members of the group have had enough time to discuss the issue so they can support the group's position, even though it may not have been their first choice. Under unanimity, all family members would fully agree with the decision.

A final way that families can make decisions is by default—that is, failure to address a pressing situation. In this situation, the decision or behavior that results is determined by a lack of attention to the issue. This is an attractive decision making option commonly employed by family businesses, especially when the issue to be resolved is very difficult or when family processes seem to immobilize any constructive problem solving.

Families may use all of these decision making styles. In fact, it is quite appropriate to use a decision making process that adequately matches the type of decision. However, in our experience, we find that families tend to use maybe one or two of these decision styles, thereby excluding all the others.

To successfully develop a transition strategy that ensures the welfare of both the family and the business, it is necessary for pertinent members of the family business to be able to discuss and come to a consensus decision clearly outlining the elements of the transition process. Therefore, it is imperative for a family business consultant to identify and assess the present skills and decision procedures currently being employed by the family. When families are able to successfully address issues and resolve these problems via consensus or unanimity, the consultant can be assured that a forum has developed in which collective decision making can occur. Inevitably, the family has some track record of success in making decisions, and the consultant should focus on this.

If decisions are primarily made by minority or majority rule, the consultant cannot be fully assured that a forum exists in which all members feel they can influence important business and family problems. Moreover, decisions made autocratically (by one individual) typically impact the overall family decision making process very negatively. In these instances, the consultant should attempt to motivate the decision maker to include the excluded family members. If the family primarily addresses decisions by default, and no track record of successful family decision making exists, the consultant must not only raise the issues that must be addressed in the family transition but teach the family how to make group decisions.

Making decisions is crucial for families engaged in developing a transition strategy for their family and business. Our experience suggests the issues listed in Table 1 on the following page require family decisions, since these issues precede or exist during succession.

One of the consultant's primary tasks in working with family business transition planning is to make sure that a forum exists in which the family as a group can make committed decisions.

■ Conflict. Families also differ in their abilities to manage the differences that arise from the complexity of closely-aligned family and business systems. Some business families can resolve conflict to the satisfaction of all family members; whereas other families may find partial resolution of their differences resulting in a degree of resentment harbored by the losing family members. It is not uncommon for business families to avoid resolving any differences they may have through open conflict, and deal with these differences behind one another's backs.

During the diagnosis phase, the consultant should assess how the family generally manages conflict, determine to what extent the family resolves differences, and note the styles of managing differences the family uses when its conflicts are *successfully* resolved. It is likely that business families that resolve conflict have established some forum in which collaboration is used as a means for resolving differences. Differences are seen as *opportunities* to solve problems. Successful procedures involve getting all family members' input and allowing each individual some say in the decision. Consultants generally attempt to help these families develop collaborative methods to resolve their differences.

**Table 1: Decisions Preceding or During Succession
That Families Must Resolve**

1. Who will be the successor, and how is one selected?
2. Who will own the company, what will be the distribution percentage across new owners, and how will individuals acquire stock?
3. What does the company mean to the family (i.e., a family employment agency, a cash cow, or is it a source of pride for the family)?
4. What is the proper time for control transfer?
5. Who will be involved in making decisions for the company in the future and how will decisions be made?
6. What role will be played by spouses?
7. What opportunities will there be for family members in the future, and under what conditions?
8. What will be the extent of the owner's involvement after the transfer control?
9. What will happen should the successor fail or become disenchanted with the business? What if two family shareholders find they cannot work together?
10. How much should we communicate to non-family members and when?
11. What will be the role of the successor? How much freedom, and what will be the limitations of his or her freedom?
12. What will be the roles of other involved family members? When are they stockholders, and when are they employees?
13. **For the current owner:** What will I do following control transfer? What mechanisms do I need to put in place to make sure the family stays together and focuses on the continued success of the business? How do I conserve family wealth? How do I keep the business from becoming an unwanted financial burden (on spouse or kids due to premature death)? How do I protect a son or daughter from siblings or other owners who may be more capable, aggressive, ambitious, etc.

Business families that have partially resolved differences typically use conflict-reducing techniques resulting in win-lose strategies, such as accommodation (giving in to another's wishes), competition (making sure your position is the one that wins), or compromise (giving a little to get a little). Business families that do not resolve their differences typically employ extreme measures to avoid communication or contact with one another.

Many reasons exist for why families avoid resolving conflict. It may be due to a history of years of open conflict, where the *real* issues were ignored rather than resolved due to personal differences; because individuals in low power positions have never been able to influence others in high power positions and have essentially given up and withdrawn; or because individuals may treat other family members with such lack of respect that there is little trust among family members to give others their due respect.

At various times, families are likely to use all three of these methods of managing their family differences. Some issues will be resolved, others partially resolved, and still some issues will have no resolution. However, it is our experience, similar to observations with family decision making, that families tend to get caught up in one of the three methods of managing differences to the neglect of the other two.

Dealing with transition planning in family businesses is synonymous with raising issues of conflict for the family to address. Our experience suggests that the conflict-laden issues of transition planning have widespread and pervasive implications for business families. (See Table 2).

Table 2: Issues That May Result in Conflict During Family Succession Planning

1. Conflict due to lack of respect or even rudeness shown toward family members in the business by the family leader.

2. Conflict over equity—business perks one gets vs. what another gets... what family members get vs. what is available to non-family...what one person contributes vs. what others contribute (e.g., especially non-family managers who have little respect for an unqualified family member as a successor or in any role).

3. General criticism about how one member deals with his/her business responsibilities or treats other family members (e.g., siblings critical of how one treats their parents).

4. Criticism of the current owner's priorities...why some things like "sales get all the resources" and "production gets leftovers."

5. Conflict due to people who wear several hats (e.g., I may talk to you as an employee (CEO) talking to an employee (Sales Manager), but you may interpret it as a father talking to a son). Other combinations:
   Shareholder ◄──► Employee
   Employer ◄──► Brother
   Family Leader ◄──► Shareholder

6. There is a role I expect my family members to play and one that they actually play (e.g., Mom's role, kids' and spouses' roles, etc.).

7. Conflict over how the business resources are tracked...managers who are non-family want accurate financial data that show the results of their labors, family wants to minimize tax.

8. Conflict between making hiring, compensation, stock distribution, financial accounting or job assignment decisions based on what one should do to help a family member vs. what one should do for the business (i.e., what is best for the family vs. what is best for the business?).

9. Conflict about what to do with the business...sell?

10. Conflict arising from the current owner transferring control in title only.

11. Conflict arising from current owner's extended vacations followed by "business-as-usual" upon his/her return.

12. Conflict about when to transfer control—current owner is reluctant and next generation is impatient.

Since resolving conflict and making decisions regarding these issues is paramount to the success of transition planning, the family business consultant must have some idea of how families will react to these transition planning issues and whether the family will be able to resolve these conflict-laden dilemmas. In those business families that have a track record of resolving conflict, the consultant may be assured that a forum exists to manage these conflicting issues. In families where partial resolution exists, the consultant knows that conflict does get addressed, but resentment may underlie much of this resolution. For those family businesses that avoid resolving conflict, the consultant must help create not only a forum to resolve conflict but be particularly sensitive in helping to create a situation with enough trust and safety that the conflict arising from the transition planning can be positively addressed.

Diagnosing Family Conflict and Decision Making Styles to Guide the Consultation

When viewed simultaneously, the style of managing conflict and making decisions of a business family may conceptually be seen as shown in the matrix displayed in Figure 1.

Figure 1: Method of Consultant Intervention in Family Businesses

| | **Decisions** | |
	One-Person Decision	Forum for Decision Involvement
Partial Resolution **Conflict**	I. Arbitrator	II. Mediator
Resolution	III. Gatekeeper/Monitor	IV. Facilitator

Furthermore, each quadrant of this matrix is suggestive of a particular style of intervention (or manner of behavior) that a consultant might use to successfully facilitate transition planning. This suggests that a consultant's role (at least initially) will change from arbitrator, to gatekeeper/monitor, to facilitator, to mediator, depending on the family's style of dealing with conflict and decisions. We will elaborate on each of these consulting roles and discuss the importance of this role for transition planning.

■ Consultant as arbitrator. When decisions are made autocratically by one family member and the family's style of dealing with conflict is partial resolution via competing/fighting methods, it behooves the consultant to intervene in the system as an arbitrator. In this role, the consultant attempts to balance the influence of all parties. He or she makes sure all the information germane to problem solving is fully elaborated and explored. He or she also keeps discussions from reaching the limits where individuals cannot hear or understand the others' points of view.

Families in this quadrant will likely express conflict openly (through their competitive style), and the one decision maker (usually the owner/founder) will likely dominate others to the greatest extent possible. Families caught in this mode will more likely than not experience difficulty in working together as a group and will attempt to avoid group meetings. Consultants working with this type of family will find it difficult to have open discussion in group meetings without conflict, and may find that working with small subsets of the group or individuals alone will be necessary.

As an arbitrator, the consultant must be more directive and should not hesitate to express his or her opinions since he or she is an expert in family business transitions. A strong relationship with the primary decision maker is required, so the consultant can disagree with this individual yet direct him or her to understand the others' positions and collectively include all the parties in the transition decisions.

■ Consultant as gatekeeper/monitor. When a family has established a forum to resolve conflict and business decisions are made primarily by one individual, the consultant should establish his or her role as a gatekeeper/monitor. This is the most helpful role in this situation because the primary obstacle to making good decisions regarding transition will result from information that is potentially available to the group, but not fully explored or made public. Hence, the consultant is needed to ensure that all points of view are expressed and shared by each individual. In addition, these families will likely have quick convergence on decisions, especially if the alternative is proposed by the primary decision maker.

Consultants might force groups to continue exploring issues and develop three or four plausible alternatives before a final decision is made. Group meetings with these families are likely to be quite harmonious, dominated by the primary decision maker. However, if the consultant does not force the family to explore all options fully, the meetings could be quite brief and the resolution will not adequately reflect a true consensus.

■ Consultant as mediator. When families have partially resolved conflict because of competing/fighting means of dealing with differences, but have established a forum for some involvement in making decisions, it is useful to intervene via a mediator role. Families employing this style typically like to meet but also like to fight. Some individuals are usually dominated by others who have developed superior skills in open competition and the *survival of the fittest* rule appears to be in operation.

In this instance, the consultant must mediate between parties to make sure decisions do not rest on the opinions of the best fighters and the level of conflict is managed. This method ensures that the dominant members are forced to hear the opinions of the less dominant and, ultimately, compromise in some manner.

■ Consultant as facilitator. When families have developed a forum where group involvement in decision making processes is used and conflicts appear to get resolved, the consultant can take on the role of facilitator. This role is perhaps the most familiar and most preferred by OD consultants, and is a role in which most consultants are highly-skilled. Also, the family that exists in this quadrant is probably more ready to deal with the complex issues of transition than those families located in any of the other three quadrants.

As a facilitator, the consultant attempts to help the family stay on track by keeping it from getting bogged down with one issue or specific data, by managing the agenda, by staying attuned to the group's process, and by using his or her unbiased third party role to add perspective and balance when needed. Consultants in this role are less likely to be concerned about the negative consequences of one dominant individual and the reluctance of the family to explore important issues in a group setting.

Group meetings with these families are usually pleasant, and there is potential for great progress to be accomplished. Although the decisions that must be addressed in transition planning will not be any less difficult for these families than those in the other three quadrants, the family processes that have been established will make the exploration of these transition issues more open to discussion and resolution.

■ Summary of consulting styles. It is fair to say that family business consultants are always trying to gradually move their clients into quadrant four, where they can embrace the role of facilitator. The consultant's ultimate goal is to educate the family and develop its skills, so it can work on tough issue with minimal consultant intervention. This appears to happen most readily when the client system has a forum to involve individuals in important decisions and the skills to resolve conflict. These conditions or attributes simply create an atmosphere conducive to developing good plans, and optimize the likelihood that there will be family commitment to the planning and implementation of the transition strategy. But family business consultants must take and accept their clients where they are and develop intervention strategies that match the client system's present level of existence.

This is similar to Harrison's advice from his classic article "Choosing the Depth of an Organizational Intervention" (reprinted in this volume). Harrison suggests that the depth of intervention be congruent with the client system's level of awareness and readiness to address the pertinent issues.

Note that the decision making process that avoids conflicts and allows for decision making by default has been deleted from our conceptual scheme in Figure 1. The reason is that the business consultant engaged in helping a client plan and manage a transition should never allow the client to deal with transition by means of avoidance or default. The mere presence of a consultant forces these issues, and it is the consultant's job to create awareness and publicly disclose the many issues of transition.

That is not to say that default and avoidance are not commonly used by families experiencing the difficulties of managing family and business concerns simultaneously. In fact, this may be one of the primary reasons that a consultant has been engaged—to aid in helping the family deal with and put into practice the many complex issues related to the transition of a business from one generation to the next. The family business consultant should always bear this in mind.

Data Collection

Sonny, did you really understand the questions that consultant was asking?

Sure did, Pop! I hope you told him what you really felt and thought. Otherwise, this is a waste of money.

Typically data is collected from interviews and sometimes questionnaires, and is aggregated and shared with the family members as well as other employees to help guide planning for the actual transition process. The objective is to create a nonthreatening forum for making family decisions concerning plans for business strategy that then can be implemented by the managers of the family business. Once this family decision making forum is established, it can be used in the future to guide the strategic direction of the family business.

With the foregoing objective and armed with our initial diagnosis of the family, we begin by collecting information from all individuals involved in the transition planning. Our interviews serve two purposes. The first is to collect valid information from all pertinent individuals that can help develop a family strategy and business strategy. The second purpose is to further clarify expectations about the intervention. Specific views about the family and about the business are categorized by the consultant and shared with the shareholders in an off-site retreat (usually a two-day meeting).

Interviews and data feedback go much like they would for other OD interventions (e.g., team building, etc.). However, our experience indicates there are a few things that family business consultants should understand. First, the level of anxiety about what is happening and what will happen with the transition planning will be far greater in family businesses than with clients from other organizations. The interview is an opportunity to alleviate some of this anxiety and to clarify expectations about how the work with the consultant will proceed.

Two common concerns often occur. One is that there is a fear that the family will invest time and energy in the transition process and nothing will get done. This is especially true when the same problems have existed for some time, and the family has successfully avoided addressing them. A second common concern is that the family wants to address the issues and get something accomplished, but certain individuals do not want to hurt anyone or be hurt (especially family members). These individuals often do not see how difficult issues can be resolved without hurting family members. Experience may dictate that addressing problem issues results in pain and anguish.

Unlike team building, it is okay to collect data from people who will not attend the planning meetings. Questionnaires completed by everyone involved plus other employees involved in organizational and business issues can be very powerful in establishing credibility for a problem. This information can be used to get the principals to face important issues they typically would categorize as nonexistent. This is also an important element for demonstrating the linkage between family issues and improvement potential of the effectiveness of the business. It is, of course, necessary to make plans for follow-up with those individuals who provided data and did not attend planning meetings.

Preparation for Planning Meetings

Mr. Consultant, I think this data you collected is a crock!

Similar to team building, it is important to meet with the boss (in this case the owner/founder) prior to any planning meeting and share the results of the data collected. In most families, everyone looks to the founder to determine early on how the planning meeting will progress. Coaching the founder prior to the family planning meeting helps others *buy into* the data, and allows their first responses to be honest representations. The consultant can then help shape this individual's response when others are present at the planning meeting. This may be very critical, especially if a tendency exists to avoid issues.

A common issue that surfaces during transition planning is lack of clarity about the roles different people will play before, during, and after the transition. Preparation of job descriptions in which a group can work during the planning meeting will make it more efficient and add legitimacy to the roles developed by the group.

Issues that are remotely related to the transition should be identified at this phase and, if necessary, categorized into separate family and business issues. Therefore, if there are family issues to be resolved, such as a dispute between the founder and spouse about the youngest son's potential role in the company, then this is an opportunity to begin working on this problem. At least, it is appropriate to distinguish this as a separate, but not entirely unrelated, issue which should be evaluated after the business issues have been resolved.

It is also important to realize that issues which are potentially great obstacles to the success of a two-day succession planning meeting will exist. For example, our experience suggests that the interpersonal interaction between father (owner) and son (chosen successor) is frequently an obstacle to this meeting. Although this pattern of interaction must be addressed by the consultant and other parties involved, changing this interaction is not always possible in a two-day retreat. However, progress can be made with steps initiated during the retreat and critical steps continued after the retreat.

For example, the following agreements may be an outcome of the planning meeting which will help begin changing the father/son pattern of interaction.

■ Both father and son recognize the critical need to change their style of relating to one another, and identify key components in the son's ability to succeed as a successor.

■ Interpersonal patterns are hard to break, and both father and son must be committed to changing this.

■ Consequences may be established and objectively administered that reward and perhaps punish father and son for relating in destructive patterns.

The Planning Meeting

So Sonny, here are the reins, take over today! You're ready, aren't you?

Come on Pop! Look at all the issues we've identified that need to be solved. Can't you be helpful?

The major steps in the planning meeting are feedback of the data, solving problems or making plans around the issues which correspond with the data, and developing specific action steps.

Feedback and Issue Refinement

Much like team building, issues are developed from "hot quotes" as organized by the consultant. Questionnaire results can also be used to further develop issues. If all goes well, the broad base of sources for the data and the consultant's coaching work with the founder (and others if necessary) will result in issues being recognized as critical and worthy of the family group dealing with them. Typically, the process the family uses now to address these issues will reflect the consultant's intervention and differ substantially from the manner the family used before.

Problem Solving

Since this format of dealing with family and business issues will likely be unfamiliar to some if not all participants, the consultant should proceed cautiously and strategically. For instance, the choice of what issue to work on first, second, and so on should be considered. A relatively easy (non-sensitive) issue should be selected first to give people an opportunity to gain some practice at the skill of problem solving and action planning. The second issue should be slightly more difficult, but its selection should depend in part on how the group performed on the first issue. The message here is not that the most sensitive issues should be saved until last. Quite the contrary, these issues should be addressed as soon as the group has gained enough experience. Otherwise, individuals will be thinking about the tough issues to come when they are working on issues taken first. Most groups need warm-up and practice interrelating and then can succeed in tackling the tough issues.

Often it is useful for another family advisor (e.g., lawyer, accountant, etc.) to be present in the planning meeting. Depending on the relationship between the family and the advisor, this person may play a key role in problem solving. Even though a group may take the issues seriously, there is a tendency for the group to not go far enough. An advisor, who has witnessed the family business tackling other issues unsuccessfully, can play a role in "holding people's feet to the fire." Without the right advisor, this may be a risky thing to do. The advisor must believe in the purpose and the design of the consultation. This advisor must also be willing to contribute the time.

Action Planning

The goal of the planning meeting is to solve problems. It is expected that some problems will not be resolved. It is likely that the consultant will recognize this during the meeting, depending on the commitment the others demonstrate during the process. What we are suggesting is that the consultant must pick and choose where and when to intervene and push. Given the luxury of time before a transition takes place, it is possible to let some of the touchy issues get by without ironclad action plans. This will give the group an opportunity to have some history with a clearly defined issue after the planning meeting, and this can be addressed more successfully during follow-up. Examples of sensitive issues are a son's ability to focus on his development of recognized weaknesses, or a father's commitment to completely delegate authority and responsibility in a particular area.

Often a problem with family businesses is accountability. Sons or daughters may demand it, but not really want it. Accountability may also be difficult to accomplish because of a parent's lack of bias when holding a son or daughter accountable in a business situation. Just like when the kids were small, the parents hold quite different views of how all other employees are held accountable. Often, it is the lack of accountability in several areas that is the problem.

Two important skills can be initiated in the planning meeting, but require follow-through documented in an action plan. One is setting the expectation for performance and following up with performance review and feedback. The second is the skill of nonthreatening and non-defensive confrontation. Both of these are very difficult in family situations that have adopted unhealthy patterns of dealing with conflict.

Follow-Up

> Well Pop, look at all we've accomplished. And the whole family is still talking to each other. Now you can take that vacation and relax.

Follow-up meetings are similar to those conducted via other OD interventions: The action plan is reviewed, and modifications are made as a result of experience with the success or lack thereof in accomplishing the tasks.

However, an important point is that follow-through may need to be sooner than is normally scheduled. The reason for this is that the pattern of the family and business may have been to avoid or deal with conflict in a way that results in just "getting by." If this occurs, these groups may quickly experience failure in key areas of the action plan. To take full advantage of the progress made in the planning meeting and the events which led up to it, it may be necessary for the consultant to stay in touch and monitor how the group is progressing, with the option of scheduling a follow-up meeting rather quickly should the need arise. Otherwise, if the family is progressing in accordance with the action plan, the follow-up meeting should convene when originally scheduled.

Conclusion

Consulting for family businesses requires special expertise. It is imperative that a family business consultant conceptually understand the complexities of the family unit and the business entity. To do so, the successful consultant must enhance both family harmony and assist the family in achieving its business goals.

References

Block, P. "The Contracting Meeting." In C.N. Jackson (ed.), *Contracting for Organization Development Consultation, Organization Development Annual, Volume II*. Alexandria, Virginia: American Society for Training and Development, 1988.

Manning, M.R. and Locke, K. "OD Contracting: Reducing Uncertainty or Creating Opportunity." In C.N. Jackson (ed.), *Contracting for Organization Development Consultation, Organization Development*

Annual, Volume II. Alexandria, Virginia: American Society for Training and Development, 1988.

McClure, S.L. "Diagnostic Selling: Why Diagnosis Comes First With the Mid-Sized Client." In C.N. Jackson and M.R. Manning (eds.), *Diagnosing Client Organizations, Organization Development Annual, Volume III.* Alexandria, Virginia: American Society for Training and Development, 1990.

Schein, E. *Process Consultation Volume I: Its Role in Organization Development,* 2d ed. Reading, Massachusetts: Addison-Wesley, 1988.

Weisbord, M. "Organizational Diagnosis: Six Places to Look for Trouble With or Without a Theory." In C.N. Jackson and M.R. Manning (eds.), *Diagnosing Client Organizations, Organization Development Annual, Volume III.* Alexandria, Virginia: American Society for Training and Development, 1990.

Part Two: Important Contributions to OD Theory and Practice

4. Intervention Theory and Method

Chris Argyris

Dr. Chris Argyis, James Bryant Conant Professor in the Graduate School of Business Administration and Education at Harvard University, is considered to be one of the founding fathers of Organization Development. In his distinguished and prolific career as a scholar, he has authored some seminal books in the OD field, including Personality and Organization *(1957),* Intervention Theory and Methods *(1970), and* Theory in Practice: Increasing Professional Effectiveness *(with Donald Schon, 1974). We are pleased to be permitted to reprint the following classic excerpt from* Intervention Theory and Methods, *which defines the key tasks of the OD consultation.*

A Definition of Intervention

To intervene is to enter into an ongoing system of relationship, to come between or among persons, groups, or objects for the purpose of helping them. There is an important implicit assumption in the definition that should be made explicit: The system exists independently of the intervenor.

There are many reasons one might wish to intervene. These reasons may range from helping the clients make their own decisions about the kind of help they need to coercing the clients to do what the intervenor wishes them to do.

Our view acknowledges interdependencies between the intervenor and the client system but focuses on how to maintain, or increase, the client system's autonomy; how to differentiate even more clearly the boundaries between the client system and the intervenor; and how to conceptualize and define the client system's health independently of the intervenor's. This view values the client system as an ongoing, self-responsible unity that has the obligation to be in control over its own destiny. An intervenor, in this view, assists a system to become more effective in problem solving, decision making, and decision implementation in such a way that the system can continue to be increasingly effective in these activities and have a decreasing need for the intervenor.

Basic Requirements for Intervention Activity

Are there any basic or necessary processes that must be fulfilled regardless of the substantive issues involved, if intervention activity is to be helpful with any level of client (individual, group, or organizational)?

One condition that seems so basic as to be defined axiomatic is the generation of *valid information*. Without valid information, it would be difficult for the client to learn and for the interventionist to help.

A second condition almost as basic flows from our assumption that intervention activity, no matter what its substantive interests and objectives, should be so designed and executed that the client system maintains its discreetness and autonomy. Thus *free, informed choice* is also a necessary process in effective intervention activity.

Finally, if the client system is assumed to be ongoing (i.e., existing over time), the clients require strengthening to maintain their autonomy not only vis-a-vis the interventionist but also vis-à-vis other systems. This means that their commitment to learning and change has to be more than temporary. It has to be so strong that it can be transferred to relationships other than those with the interventionist and can do so (eventually) without the help of the interventionist. The third basic process for any intervention activity is, therefore, the client's *internal commitment* to the choices made.

In summary, valid information, free choice, and internal commitment are considered integral parts of any intervention activity, no matter what the substantive objectives are (e.g., developing a management performance evaluation scheme, reducing intergroup rivalries, increasing the degree of trust among individuals, redesigning budgetary systems, or redesigning work). These three processes are called the primary intervention tasks.

Primary Tasks of an Interventionist

Why is it necessary to hypothesize that in order for an interventionist to behave effectively, and in order that the integrity of the client system be maintained, the interventionist has to focus on three primary tasks, regardless of the substantive problems that the client system may be experiencing?

Valid and Useful Information

First, it has been accepted as axiomatic that valid and useful information is the foundation for effective intervention. Valid information is that which describes the factors, plus their interrelationships, that create the problem for the client system.

There are several tests for checking the validity of the information. In increasing degrees of power they are public verifiability, valid prediction, and control over the phenomena. The first is having several independent diagnoses suggest the same picture. Second is generating predictions from the diagnosis that are subsequently confirmed (they occurred under the conditions that were specified). Third is altering the factors systematically and predicting the effects upon the system as a whole.

All these tests, if they are to be valid, must be carried out in such a way that the participants cannot, at will, make them come true. This would be a self-fulfilling prophecy and not a confirmation of a prediction. The difficulty with a self-fulfilling prophecy is its indication of more about the degree of power an individual (or subset of individuals) can muster to alter the system than about the nature of the system when the participants are behaving without knowledge of the diagnosis.

For example, if an executive learns that the interventionist predicts his subordinates will behave (a) if he behaves (b), he might alter (b) in order not to lead to (a). Such an alteration indicates the executive's power but does not test the validity of the diagnosis that if (a), then (b).

The tests for valid information have important implications for effective intervention activity. First, the interventionist's diagnoses must strive to represent the total client system and not the point of view of any subgroup or individual. Otherwise, the interventionist could not be seen only as being under the control of a particular individual or subgroup, but also his predictions would be based upon inaccurate information and thus might not be confirmed.

This does not mean that an interventionist may not begin with, or may not limit his relationship to, a subpart of the total system. It is totally possible, for example, for the interventionist to help management, blacks, trade union leaders, etc. With whatever subgroup he works, he simply should not agree to limit his diagnosis to its wishes.

It is conceivable that a client system may be helped even though valid information is not generated. Sometimes changes occur in a positive direction without the interventionist having played any important role. These changes, although helpful in that specific instance, lack the attribute of helping the organization to learn to gain control over its problem-solving capability.

The importance of information that the clients can use to control their destiny points up the requirement that the information must not only be valid, it must be useful. Valid information that cannot be used by the clients to alter their system is equivalent to valid information about cancer that cannot be used to cure cancer eventually. An interventionist's diagnosis should include variables that are manipulable by the clients and are complete enough so that if they are manipulated, effective change will follow.

Free Choice

In order to have free choice, the client has to have a cognitive map of what he wishes to do. The objectives of his action are known at the moment of decision. Free choice implies voluntary as opposed to automatic; proactive rather than reactive. The act of selection is rarely accomplished by maximizing or optimizing. Free and informed choice entails what Simon has called "satisficing;" that is, selecting the alternative with the highest probability of succeeding, given some specified cost constraints. Free choice places the locus of decision making in the client system. Free choice makes it possible for the clients to remain responsible for their destiny. Through free choice, the clients can maintain the autonomy of their system.

It may be possible that clients prefer to give up their responsibility and their autonomy, especially if they are feeling a sense of failure. They may prefer, as we shall see in several examples, to turn over their free choice to the interventionist. They may insist that he make recommendations and tell them what to do. The interventionist resists these pressures because if he does not, the clients will lose their free choice and he will lose his own free choice also. He will be controlled by the anxieties of the clients.

The requirement of free choice is especially important for those helping activities where the processes of help are as important as the actual help. For example, a medical doctor does not require that a patient with a bullet wound participate in the process by defining the kind of help he needs. However, the same doctor may have to pay much more attention to the processes he uses to help patients when he is attempting to diagnose blood pressure or cure a high cholesterol. If the doctor behaves in ways that upset the patient, the latter's blood pressure may well be distorted. Or, the patient can develop a dependent relationship if the doctor cuts down his cholesterol—increasing habits only under constant pressure from the doctor—and the moment the relationship is broken off, the count goes up.

Effective intervention in the human and social sphere requires that the processes of help be congruent with the outcome desired. Free choice is important because there are so many unknowns, and the interventionist wants the client to have as much willingness and motivation as possible to work on the problem. With high client motivation and commitment, several different methods for change can succeed.

A choice is free to the extent the members can make their selection for a course of action with minimal internal defensiveness; can define the path (or paths) by which the intended consequence is to be achieved; can relate the choice to their central needs; and can build into their choices a realistic and challenging level of aspiration. Free choice, therefore, implies that the members are able to explore as many alternatives as they consider significant and select those that are central to their needs.

Why must the choice be related to the central needs, and why must the level of aspiration be realistic and challenging? May people not choose freely unrealistic or unchallenging objectives? Yes, they may do so in the short-run, but not for long if they still want to have free and informed choice. A freely chosen course of action means that the action must be based on an accurate analysis of the situation and not on the biases or defenses of the decision makers. We know, from the level of aspiration studies, that choices which are too high or too low, which are too difficult or not difficult enough will tend to lead to psychological failure.

Psychological failure will lead to increased defensiveness, increased failure, and decreased self-acceptance on the part of the members experiencing the failure. These conditions, in turn, will tend to lead to distorted perceptions by the members making the choices. Moreover, the defensive members may unintentionally create a climate where the members of surrounding and interrelated systems will tend to provide carefully censored information. Choices made under these conditions are neither informed nor free.

Turning to the question of centrality of needs, a similar logic applies. The degree of commitment to the processes of generating valid information, scanning, and choosing may significantly vary according to the centrality of the choice to the needs of the clients. The more central the choice, the more the system will strive to do its best in developing valid information and making free and informed choices. If the research from perceptual psychology is valid, the very perception of the clients is altered by the needs involved.

Individuals tend to scan more, ask for more information, and be more careful in their choices when they are making decisions that are central to them. High involvement may produce perceptual distortions, as does low involvement. The interventionist, however, may have a greater probability of helping the clients explore possible distortions when the choice they are making is a critical one.

Internal Commitment

Internal commitment means that course of action or choice that has been internalized by each member so that he experiences a high degree of ownership and has a feeling of responsibility about the choice and its implications. Internal commitment means that individual has reached the point where he is acting on the choice because it fulfills his own needs and sense of responsibility, as well as those of the system.

The individual who is internally committed is acting primarily under the influence of his own forces and not induced forces. The individual (or any unity) feels a minimal degree of dependence upon others for the action. It implies that he has obtained and processed valid information and that he has made an informed and free choice. Under these conditions, there is a high probability that the individual's commitment will remain strong over time (even with reduction of external rewards) or under stress, or when the course of action is challenged by others. It also implies that the individual is continually open to reexamination of his position because he believes in taking action based upon valid information.

Reference

Chris Argyris. *Intervention Theory and Methods: A Behavioral Science View.* Reading, Massachusetts: Addison-Wesley Publishing, 1970.

5. Choosing the Depth of Organizational Intervention

Roger Harrison

Dr. Roger Harrison has long been a pioneer and leader in the field of Organization Development. A former faculty member at Yale University, he has spent the last two decades as an active consultant in the U.S. and abroad. Now consulting out of Mountain View, California (Harrison Associates), he also continues to make intellectual contributions to the OD literature. We are pleased to be permitted to reprint the following classic article from his earlier writings, which addresses important issues relevant to both effective intervention methods and consultant ethics.

Since World War II there has been a great proliferation of behavioral science-based methods by which consultants seek to facilitate growth and change in individuals, groups, and organizations. The methods range from operations analysis and manipulation of the organization chart, through the use of Grid laboratories, T-groups, and nonverbal techniques. As was true in the development of clinical psychology and psychotherapy, the early stages of this developmental process tend to be accompanied by considerable competition, criticism, and argument about the relative merits of various approaches.

It is my conviction that controversy over the relative goodness or badness, effectiveness or ineffectiveness, of various change strategies really accomplishes very little in the way of increased knowledge or unification of behavioral science. As long as we are arguing about what method is better than another, we tend to learn very little about how various approaches fit together or complement one another, and we certainly make more difficult and ambiguous the task of bringing these competing points of view within one overarching system of knowledge about human processes.

As our knowledge increases, it begins to be apparent that these competing change strategies are not really different ways of doing the same thing — some more effective and some less effective — but rather that they are different ways of doing *different* things. They touch the individual, the group, or the organization in different aspects of their functioning. They require differing kinds and amounts of commitment on the part of the client for them to be successful, and they demand different varieties and levels of skills and abilities on the part of the practitioner.

I believe that there is a real need for conceptual models which differentiate intervention strategies from one another in a way which permits rational matching of strategies to organizational change problems. The purpose of this paper is to present a modest beginning which I have made toward a conceptualization of strategies, and to derive from this conceptualization some criteria for choosing appropriate methods of intervention in particular applications.

The point of view of this paper is that the depth of individual emotional involvement in the change process can be a central concept for differentiating change strategies. In focusing on this dimension, we are concerned with the extent to which core areas of the personality or self are the focus of the change attempt.

Strategies which touch the more deep, personal, private, and central aspects of the individual or his relationships with others fall toward the deeper end of this continuum. Strategies which deal with more external aspects of the individual and which focus upon the more formal and public aspects of role behavior tend to fall toward the surface end of the depth dimension. This dimension has the advantage that it is relatively easy to rank change strategies upon it and to get fairly close consensus as to the ranking. It is a widely discussed dimension of difference which has meaning and relevance to practitioners and their clients.

I hope in this paper to promote greater flexibility and rationality in choosing appropriate depths of intervention. I shall approach this task by examining the effects of interventions at various depths. I shall also explore the ways in which two important organizational processes tend to make demands and to set limits upon the depth of intervention which can produce effective change in organizational functioning. These two processes are the autonomy of organization members and their own perception of their needs for help.

Before illustrating the concept by ranking five common intervention strategies along the dimension of depth, I should like to define the dimension somewhat more precisely. We are concerned essentially with how private, individual, and hidden are the issues and processes about which the consultant attempts directly to obtain information and which he seeks to influence. If the consultant seeks information about relatively public and observable aspects of behavior and relationships, and if he tries to influence directly only these relatively surface characteristics and processes, we would then categorize his intervention strategy as being closer to the surface. If, on the other hand, the consultant seeks information about very deep and private perceptions, attitudes, or feelings, and if he intervenes in a way which directly affects these processes, then we would classify his intervention strategy as one of considerable depth.

To illustrate the surface end of the dimension, let us look first at operations research or operations analysis. This strategy is concerned with the roles and functions to be performed within the organization, generally with little regard to the individual characteristics of persons occupying the roles. The change strategy is to manipulate role relationships; in other words, to redistribute the tasks, the resources, and the relative power attached to various roles in the organization. This is essentially a process of rational analysis in which the tasks which need to be performed are determined and specified, and then sliced up into role definitions for persons and groups in the organization.

The operations analyst does not ordinarily need to know much about particular people. Indeed, his function is to design the organization in such a way that its successful operation does not depend too heavily upon any uniquely individual skills, abilities, values, or attitudes of persons in various roles. He may perform this function adequately without knowing in advance who the people are who will fill these slots. Persons are assumed to be moderately interchangeable and, in order to make this approach work, it is necessary to design the organization so that the capabilities, needs, and values of the individual which are relevant to role performance are relatively public and observable, and are possessed by a fairly large proportion of the population from which organization members are drawn. The approach is certainly one of very modest depth.

Somewhat deeper are those strategies which are based upon evaluating individual performance and attempting to manipulate it directly. Included in this approach is much of the industrial psychologist's work in selection, placement, appraisal, and counseling of employees. The intervener is concerned with what the individual is able and likely to do and achieve rather than with processes internal to the individual. Direct attempts to influence performance may be made through the application of rewards and punishments such as promotions, salary increases, or transfers within the organization.

An excellent illustration of this focus on end results is the practice of management by objectives. The intervention process is focused on establishing mutually agreed-upon goals for performance between the individual and his supervisor. The practice is considered to be particularly advantageous because it permits the supervisor to avoid a focus on personal characteristics of the subordinate, particularly those deeper, more central characteristics which managers generally have difficulty in discussing with those who work under their supervision. The process is designed to limit information exchange to that which is public and observable, such as the setting of performance goals and the success or failure of the individual in attaining them.

Because of its focus on end results, rather than on the process by which those results are achieved, management by objectives must be considered less deep than the broad area of concern with work style which I shall term instrumental process analysis. We are concerned here not only with performance but with the processes by which that performance is achieved. However, we are primarily concerned with styles and processes of work rather than with the processes of interpersonal relationships which I would classify as being deeper on the basic dimension.

In instrumental process analysis, we are concerned with how a person likes to organize and conduct his work, and with the impact which this style of work has on others in the organization. Principally, we are concerned with how a person perceives his role, what he values and disvalues in it, and what he works hard on and what he chooses to ignore. We are also interested in the instrumental acts which the individual directs toward others: delegating authority or reserving decisions to himself; communicating or withholding information; collaborating or competing with others on work-related issues. The focus on instrumentality means that we are interested in the person primarily as a doer of work or a performer of functions related to the goals of the organization. We are interested in what facilitates or inhibits his effective task performance.

We are not interested per se in whether his relationships with others are happy or unhappy, whether they perceive him as too warm or too cold, too authoritarian or too laissez-faire, or any other of the many interpersonal relationships which arise as people associate in organizations. However, I do not mean to imply that the line between instrumental relationships and interpersonal ones is an easy one to draw in action and practice, or even that it is desirable that this be done.

Depth Gauges: Level of Tasks and Feelings

What I am saying is that an intervention strategy can focus on instrumentality or it can focus on interpersonal relationships, and that there are important consequences of this difference in depth of intervention.

When we intervene at the level of instrumentality, it is to change work behavior and working relationships. Frequently this involves the process of bargaining or negotiation between groups and individuals. Diagnoses are made of the satisfactions or dissatisfactions of organization members with one another's work behavior. Reciprocal adjustments, bargains, and trade-offs can then be arranged in which each party gets some modification in the behavior of the other at the cost to him of some reciprocal accommodation. Much of the intervention strategy which has been developed around Blake's concept of the Managerial Grid is at this level and involves bargaining and negotiation of role behavior as an important change process.

At the deeper level of interpersonal relationships, the focus is on feelings, attitudes, and perceptions which organization members have about others. At this level we are concerned with the quality of human relationships within the organization, with warmth and coldness of members to one another, and with the experiences of acceptance and rejection, love and hate, trust and suspicion among groups and individuals. At this level the consultant probes for normally hidden feelings, attitudes, and perceptions. He works to create relationships of openness about feelings and to help members to develop mutual understanding of one another as persons. Interventions are directed toward helping organization members to be more comfortable in being authentically themselves with one another, and the degree of mutual caring and concern is expected to increase.

Sensitivity training using T-groups is a basic intervention strategy at this level. T-group educators emphasize increased personalization of relationships, the development of trust and openness, and the exchange of feelings. Interventions at this level deal directly and intensively with interpersonal emotionality. This is the first intervention strategy we have examined which is at a depth where the feelings of organization members about one another as persons are a direct focus of the intervention strategy.

At the other levels, such feelings certainly exist and may be expressed, but they are not a direct concern of the intervention. The transition from the task orientation of instrumental process analysis to the feeling orientation of interpersonal process analysis seems, as I shall suggest later, to be a critical one for many organization members.

The deepest level of intervention which will be considered in this paper is that of intrapersonal analysis. Here the consultant uses a variety of methods to reveal the individual's deeper attitudes, values, and conflicts regarding his own functioning, identity, and existence. The focus is generally on increasing the range of experiences which the individual can bring into awareness and cope with. The material may be dealt with at the fantasy or symbolic level, and the intervention strategies include many which are non-interpersonal and nonverbal. Some examples of this approach are the use of marathon T-group sessions, the creative risk-taking laboratory approach of Byrd (1967), and some aspects of the task group therapy approach of Clark (1966). These approaches all tend to bring into focus very deep and intense feelings about one's own identity and one's relationships with significant others.

Although I have characterized deeper interventions as dealing increasingly with the individual's affective life, I do not imply that issues at less deep levels may not be emotionally charged. Issues of role differentiation, reward distribution, and ability and performance evaluation, for example, are frequently invested with strong feelings. The concept of depth is concerned more with the *accessibility* and *individuality* of attitudes, values, and perceptions than it is with their strength. This narrowing of the common usage of the term *depth* is necessary to avoid the contradictions which occur when strength and inaccessibility are confused. For instance, passionate value confrontation and bitter conflict have frequently occurred between labor and management over economic issues which are surely toward the surface end of my concept of depth.

In order to understand the importance of the concept of depth for choosing interventions in organizations, let us consider the effects upon organization members of working at different levels.

The first of the important concomitants of depth is the degree of dependence of the client on the special competence of the change agent. At the surface end of the depth dimension, the methods of intervention are easily communicated and made public. The client may reasonably expect to learn something of the change agent's skills to improve his own practice. At the deeper levels, such as interpersonal and intrapersonal process analyses, it is more difficult for the client to understand the methods of intervention. The change agent is more likely to be seen as a person of special and unusual powers not found in ordinary men. Skills of intervention and change are less frequently learned by organization members, and the change process may tend to become personalized around the change agent as leader. Programs of change which are so dependent upon personal relationships and individual expertise are difficult to institutionalize. When the change agent leaves the system, he may not only take his expertise with him but the entire change process as well.

A second aspect of the change process which varies with depth is the extent to which the benefits of an intervention are transferable to members of the organization not originally participating in the change process. At surface levels of operations analysis and performance evaluation, the effects are institutionalized in the form of procedures, policies, and practices of the organization which may have considerable permanence beyond the tenure of individuals. At the level of instrumental behavior, the continuing effects of intervention are more likely to reside in the informal norms of groups within the organization regarding such matters as delegation, communication, decision making, competition and collaboration, and conflict resolution.

At the deepest levels of intervention, the target of change is the individual's inner life; and if the intervention is successful, the permanence of individual change should be greatest. There are indeed dramatic reports of cases in which persons have changed their careers and life goals as a result of such interventions, and the persistence of such change appears to be relatively high.

One consequence, then, of the level of intervention is that with greater depth of focus, the individual increasingly becomes both the target and the carrier of change. In the light of this analysis, it is not surprising to observe that deeper levels of intervention are increasingly being used at higher organizational levels and in scientific and service organizations where the contribution of the individual has greatest impact.

An important concomitant of depth is that as the level of intervention becomes deeper, the information needed to intervene effectively becomes less available. At the less personal level of operations analysis, the information is often a matter of record. At the level of performance evaluation, it is a matter of observation. On the other hand, reactions of others to a person's work style are less likely to be discussed freely, and the more personal responses to his interpersonal style are even less likely to be readily given. At the deepest levels, important information may not be available to the individual himself. Thus, as we go deeper, the consultant must use more of his time and skill uncovering information which is ordinarily private and hidden. This is one reason for the greater costs of interventions at deeper levels of focus.

Another aspect of the change process which varies with the depth of intervention is the personal risk and unpredictability of outcome for the individual. At deeper levels we deal with aspects of the individual's view of himself and his relationships with others, which are relatively untested by exposure to the evaluations and emotional reactions of others. If in the change process the individual's self-perceptions are strongly disconfirmed, the resulting imbalance in internal forces may produce sudden changes in behavior, attitudes, and personality integration.

Because of the private and hidden nature of the processes into which we intervene at deeper levels, it is difficult to predict the individual impact of the change process in advance. The need for clinical sensitivity and skill on the part of the practitioner thus increases, since he must be prepared to diagnose and deal with developing situations involving considerable stress upon individuals.

The foregoing analysis suggests a criterion by which to match intervention strategies to particular organizational problems. It is *to intervene at a level no deeper than that required to produce enduring solutions to the problems at hand.* This criterion derives directly from the observations above. The cost, skill demands, client dependency, and variability of outcome all increase with depth of intervention. Further, as the depth of intervention increases, the effects tend to locate more in the individual and less in the organization. The danger of losing the organization's investment in the change with the departure of the individual becomes a significant consideration.

Autonomy Increases Depth of Intervention

While this general criterion is simple and straightforward, its application is not. In particular, although the criterion should operate in the direction of less depth of intervention, there is a general trend in modern organizational life which tends to push the intervention level ever deeper. This trend is toward increased self-direction of organization members and increased independence of external pressures and incentives. I believe that there is a direct relationship between the autonomy of individuals and the depth of intervention needed to effect organizational change.

Before going on to discuss this relationship, I shall acknowledge freely that I cannot prove the existence of a trend toward a general increase in freedom of individuals within organizations. I intend only to assert the great importance of the degree of individual autonomy in determining the level of intervention which will be effective.

In order to understand the relationship between autonomy and depth of intervention, it is necessary to conceptualize a dimension which parallels and is implied by the depth dimension we have been discussing. This is the dimension of predictability and variability among persons in their responses to the different kinds of incentives which may be used to influence behavior in the organization. The key assumption in this analysis is that the more unpredictable and unique is the individual's response to the particular kinds of controls and incentives one can bring to bear upon him, the more one must know about that person in order to influence his behavior.

Most predictable and least individual is the response of the person to economic and bureaucratic controls when his needs for economic income and security are high. It is not necessary to delve very deeply into a person's inner processes in order to influence his behavior if we know that he badly needs his income and his position and if we are in a position to control his access to these rewards. Responses to economic and bureaucratic controls tend to be relatively simple and on the surface.

Independence of Economic Incentive

If for any reason organization members become relatively uninfluenceable through the manipulation of their income and economic security, the management of performance becomes strikingly more complex; and the need for more personal information about the individual increases. Except very generally, we do not know automatically or in advance what styles of instrumental or interpersonal interaction will be responded to as negative or positive incentives by the individual. One person may appreciate close supervision and direction; another may value independence of direction. One may prefer to work alone; another may function best when he is in close communication with others. One may thrive in close, intimate, personal interaction; while others are made uncomfortable by any but cool and distant relationships with colleagues.

What I am saying is that when bureaucratic and economic incentives lose their force for whatever reason, the improvement of performance *must* involve linking organizational goals to the individual's attempts to meet his own needs for satisfying instrumental activities and interpersonal relationships. It is for this reason that I make the assertion that increases in personal autonomy dictate change interventions at deeper and more personal levels. In order to obtain the information necessary to link organizational needs to individual goals, one must probe fairly deeply into the attitudes, values, and emotions of the organization members.

If the need for deeper personal information becomes great when we intervene at the instrumental and interpersonal levels, it becomes even greater when one is dealing with organization members who are motivated less through their transactions with the environment and more in response to internal values and standards. An example is the researcher, engineer, or technical specialist whose work behavior may be influenced more by his own values and standards of creativity or professional excellence than by his relationships with others. The deepest organizational interventions at the intrapersonal level may be required in order to effect change when working with persons who are highly self-directed.

Let me summarize my position about the relationship among autonomy, influence, and level of intervention. As the individual becomes less subject to economic and bureaucratic pressures, he tends to seek more intangible rewards in the organization which come from both the instrumental and interpersonal aspects of the system. I view this as a shift from greater external to more internal control and as an increase in autonomy. Further shifts in this direction may involve increased independence of rewards and punishments mediated by others, in favor of operation in accordance with internal values and standards.

I view organizations as systems of reciprocal influence. Achievement of organization goals is facilitated when individuals can seek their own satisfactions through activity which promotes the goals of the organization. As the satisfactions which are of most value to the individual change, so must the reciprocal influence systems, if the organization goals are to continue to be met.

If the individual changes are in the direction of increased independence of external incentives, then the influence systems must change to provide opportunities for individuals to achieve more intangible, self-determined satisfactions in their work. However, people are more differentiated, complex, and unique in their intangible goals and values than in their economic needs. In order to create systems which offer a wide variety of intangible satisfactions, much more private information about individuals is needed than is required to create and maintain systems based chiefly on economic and bureaucratic controls. For this reason, deeper interventions are called for when the system which they would attempt to change contains a high proportion of relatively autonomous individuals.

There are a number of factors promoting autonomy, all tending to free the individual from dependence upon economic and bureaucratic controls, which I have observed in my work with organizations. Wherever a number of these factors obtain, it is probably an indication that deeper levels of intervention are required to effect lasting improvements in organizational functioning. I shall simply list these indicators briefly in categories to show what kinds of things might signify to the practitioner that deeper levels of intervention may be appropriate.

The first category includes anything which makes the evaluation of individual performance difficult:

■ A long time span between the individual's actions and the results by which effectiveness of performance is to be judged.

■ Non-repetitive, unique tasks which cannot be evaluated by reference to the performance of others on similar tasks.

■ Specialized skills and abilities possessed by an individual which cannot be evaluated by a supervisor who does not possess the skills or knowledge himself.

The second category concerns economic conditions:

■ Arrangements which secure the job tenure and/or income of the individual.

■ A market permitting easy transfer from one organization to another (e.g., engineers in the United States aerospace industry).

■ Unique skills and knowledge of the individual which make him difficult to replace.

The third category includes characteristics of the system or its environment which lead to independence of the parts of the organization and decentralization of authority such as:

■ An organization which works on a project basis instead of producing a standard line of products.

■ An organization in which subparts must be given latitude to deal rapidly and flexibly with frequent environmental change.

I should like to conclude the discussion of this criterion for depth of intervention with a brief reference to the ethics of intervention: a problem which merits considerably more thorough treatment than I can give it here.

The Ethics of Delving Deeper

There is considerable concern in the United States about invasion of privacy by behavioral scientists. I would agree that such invasion of privacy is an actual as well as a fantasied concomitant of the use of organizational change strategies of greater depth. The recourse by organizations to such strategies has been widely viewed as an indication of greater organizational control over the most personal and private aspects of the lives of the members. The present analysis suggests, however, that recourse to these deeper interventions actually reflects the greater *freedom* of organization members from traditionally crude and impersonal means of organizational control.

There is no reason to be concerned about man's attitudes or values or interpersonal relationships when his job performance can be controlled by brute force, by economic coercion, or by bureaucratic rules and regulations. The "invasion of privacy" becomes worth the cost, bother, and uncertainty of outcome only when the individual has achieved relative independence from control by other means. Put another way, it makes organizational sense to try to get a man to *want* to do something only if you cannot *make* him do it. And regardless of what intervention strategy is used, the individual still retains considerably greater control over his own behavior than he had when he could be manipulated more crudely.

As long as we can maintain a high degree of voluntarism regarding the nature and extent of an individual's participation in the deeper organizational change strategies, these strategies can work toward adapting the organization to the individual quite as much as they work the other way around. Only when an individual's participation in one of the deeper change strategies is coerced by economic or bureaucratic pressures, do I feel that the ethics of the intervention clearly run counter to the values of a democratic society.

Role of Client Norms and Values in Determining Depth

So far our attention to the choice of level of intervention has focused upon locating the depth at which the information exists which must be exchanged to facilitate system improvement. Unfortunately, the choice of an intervention strategy cannot practically be made with reference to this criterion alone. Even if a correct diagnosis is made of the level at which the relevant information lies, we may not be able to work effectively at the desired depth because of client norms, values, resistances, and fears.

In an attempt to develop a second criterion for depth of intervention which takes such dispositions on the part of the client into account, I have considered two approaches which represent polarized orientations to the problem. One approach is based upon analyzing and overcoming client resistance; the other is based upon discovering and joining forces with the self-articulated wants or "felt needs" of the client.

There are several ways of characterizing these approaches. To me, the simplest is to point out that when the change agent is resistance-oriented he tends to lead or influence the client to work at a depth greater than that at which the latter feels comfortable. When resistance-oriented, the change agent tends to mistrust the client's statement of his problems and of the areas where he wants help. He suspects the client's presentation of being a smoke screen or defense against admission of his "real" problems and needs. The consultant works to expose the underlying processes and concerns and to influence the client to work at a deeper level. The resistance-oriented approach grows out of the work of clinicians and psychotherapists, and it characterizes much of the work of organizational consultants who specialize in sensitivity training and deeper intervention strategies.

On the other hand, change agents may be oriented to the self-articulated needs of clients. When so oriented, the consultant tends more to follow and facilitate the client in working at whatever level the latter sets for himself. He may assist the client in defining problems and needs and in working on solutions, but he is inclined to try to anchor his work in the norms, values, and accepted standards of behavior of the organization.

I believe that there is a tendency for change agents working at the interpersonal and deeper levels to adopt a rather consistent resistance-oriented approach. Consultants so oriented seem to take a certain quixotic pride in dramatically and self-consciously violating organizational norms. Various techniques have been developed for pressuring or seducing organizations members into departing from organizational norms in the service of change. The "marathon" T-group is a case in point, where the increased irritability and fatigue of prolonged contact and lack of sleep move participants to deal with one another more emotionally, personally, and spontaneously than they would normally be willing to do.

I suspect that unless such norm-violating intervention efforts actually succeed in changing organizational norms, their effects are relatively short-lived, because the social structures and interpersonal linkages have not been created which can utilize for day-to-day problem solving the deeper information produced by the intervention. It is true that the consultant may succeed in producing information, but he is less likely to succeed in creating social structures which can continue to work in his absence.

The problem is directly analogous to that of the community developer who succeeds by virtue of his personal influence in getting villagers to build a school or a community center which falls into disuse as soon as he leaves because of the lack of any integration of these achievements into the social structure and day-to-day needs and desires of the community. Community developers have had to learn through bitter failure and frustration that ignoring or subverting the standards and norms of a social system often results in temporary success followed by a reactionary increase in resistance to the influence of the change agent.

On the other hand, felt needs embody those problems, issues, and difficulties which have a high conscious priority on the part of community or organization members. We can expect individuals and groups to be ready to invest time, energy, and resources in dealing with their felt needs, while they will be relatively passive or even resistant toward those who attempt to help them with externally defined needs. Community developers have found that attempts to help with felt needs are met with greater receptivity, support, and integration within the structure and life of the community than are intervention attempts which rely primarily upon the developer's value system for setting need priorities.

The emphasis of many organizational change agents on confronting and working through resistances was developed originally in the practice of individual psychoanalysis and psychotherapy, and it is also a central concept in the conduct of therapy groups and sensitivity training laboratories. In all of these situations, the change agent has a high degree of environmental control and is at least temporarily in a high status position with respect to the client. To a degree that is frequently underestimated by practitioners, we manage to create a situation in which it is more unpleasant for the client to leave than it is to stay and submit to the pressure to confront and work through resistances. I believe that the tendency is for behavioral scientists to overplay their hands when they move from the clinical and training situations where they have environmental control to the organizational consulting situation, where their control is sharply attenuated.

This attenuation derives only partially from the relative ease with which the client can terminate the relationship. Even if this most drastic step is not taken, the consultant can be tolerated, misled, and deceived in ways which are relatively difficult in the therapeutic or human relations training situations. He can also be openly defied and blocked if he runs afoul of strongly shared group norms; whereas when the consultant is dealing with a group of strangers, he can often utilize differences among the members to overcome this kind of resistance.

I suspect that, in general, behavioral scientists underestimate their power in working with individuals and groups of strangers, and overestimate it when working with individuals and groups in organizations. I emphasize this point because I believe that a good many potentially fruitful and mutually satisfying consulting relationships are terminated early because of the consultant's taking the role of overcomer of resistance to change rather than that of collaborator in the client's attempts at solving his problems. It is these considerations which lead me to suggest my second criterion for the choice of organization intervention strategy: *to intervene at a level no deeper than that at which the energy and resources of the client can be committed to problem solving and to change.* These energies and resources can be mobilized through obtaining legitimation for the intervention in the norms of the organization and through devising intervention strategies which have clear relevance to consciously felt needs on the part of the organization members.

The Consultant's Dilemma: Felt Needs Versus Deeper Levels

Unfortunately, it is doubtlessly true that the forces which influence the conditions we desire to change often exist at deeper levels than can be dealt with by adhering to the criterion of working within organization norms and meeting felt needs. The level at which an individual or group is willing and ready to invest energy and resources is probably always determined partly by a realistic assessment of the problems and partly by a defensive need to avoid confrontation and significant change. It is thus not likely that our two criteria for selection of intervention depth will result in the same decisions when practically applied. It is not the same to intervene at the level where behavior-determining forces are most potent as it is to work on felt needs as they are articulated by the client. This, it seems to me, is the consultant's dilemma. It always has been. We are continually faced with the choice between leading the client into areas which are threatening, unfamiliar, and dependency-provoking for him (and where our own expertise shows up to best advantage) or, on the other hand, being guided by the client's own understanding of his problems and his willingness to invest resources in particular kinds of relatively familiar and nonthreatening strategies.

When time permits, this dilemma is ideally dealt with by intervening first at a level where there is good support from the norms, power structure, and felt needs of organizational members. The consultant can then, over a period of time, develop trust, sophistication, and support within the organization to explore deeper levels at which particularly important forces may be operating. This would probably be agreed to, at least in principle, by most organizational consultants.

The point at which I feel I differ from a significant number of workers in this field is that I would advocate that interventions should *always* be limited to the depth of the client's felt needs and readiness to legitimize intervention. I believe we should always avoid moving deeper at a pace which outstrips a client system's willingness to subject itself to exposure, dependency, and threat. What I am saying is that if the dominant response of organization members indicates that an intervention violates system norms regarding exposure, privacy, and confrontation, then one has intervened too deeply and should pull back to a level at which organization members are more ready to invest their own energy in the change process.

This point of view is thus in opposition to that which sees negative reactions primarily as indications of resistances which are to be brought out into the open, confronted, and worked through as a central part of the intervention process. I believe that behavioral scientists acting as organizational consultants have tended to place overmuch emphasis on the overcoming of resistance to change and have underemphasized the importance of enlisting in the service of change the energies and resources which the client can consciously direct and willingly devote to problem solving.

What is advocated here is that we in general accept the client's felt needs or the problems he presents as real and that we work on them at a level at which he can serve as a competent and willing collaborator. This position is in opposition to one which sees the presenting problem as more or less a smoke screen or barrier. I am not advocating this point of view because I value the right to privacy of organization members more highly than I value their growth and development or the solution of organizational problems. (This is an issue which concerns me, but it is enormously more complex than the ones with which I am dealing in this paper.) Rather, I place first priority on collaboration with the client, because I do not think we are frequently successful consultants without it.

In my own practice I have observed that the change in client response is frequently quite striking when I move from a resistance-oriented approach to an acceptance of the client's norms and definitions of his own needs. With quite a few organizational clients in the United States, the line of legitimacy seems to lie somewhere between interventions at the instrumental level and those focused on interpersonal relationships. Members who exhibit hostility, passivity, and dependence when I initiate intervention at the interpersonal level may become dramatically more active, collaborative, and involved when I shift the focus to the instrumental level.

If I intervene directly at the level of interpersonal relationships, I can be sure that at lease some members, and often the whole group, will react with anxiety, passive resistance, and low or negative commitment to the change process. Furthermore, they express their resistance in terms of norms and values regarding the appropriateness or legitimacy of dealing at this level. They say things like, "It isn't right to force people's feelings about one another out into the open;" "I don't see what this has to do with improving organizational effectiveness;" and "People are being encouraged to say things which are better left unsaid."

If I then switch to a strategy which focuses on decision making, delegation of authority, information exchange, and other instrumental questions, these complaints about illegitimacy and the inappropriateness of the intervention are usually sharply reduced. This does not mean that the clients are necessarily comfortable or free from anxiety in the discussions, nor does it mean that strong feelings may not be expressed about one another's behavior. What is different is that the clients are more likely to *work with* instead of *against* me, to feel and express some sense of ownership in the change process, and to see many more possibilities for carrying it on among themselves in the absence of the consultant.

What I have found is that when I am resistance-oriented in my approach to the client, I am apt to feel rather uncomfortable in "letting sleeping dogs lie." When, on the other hand, I orient myself to the client's own assessment of his needs, I am uncomfortable when I feel I am leading or pushing the client to operate very far outside the shared norms of the organization. I have tried to indicate why I believe the latter orientation is more appropriate. I realize of course that many highly sophisticated and talented practitioners will not agree with me.

In summary, I have tried to show in this paper that the dimension of depth should be central to the conceptualization of intervention strategies. I have presented what I believe are the major consequences of intervening at greater or lesser depths, and from these consequences I have suggested two criteria for choosing the appropriate depth of intervention: first, *to intervene at a level no deeper than that required to produce enduring solutions to the problems at hand;* and second, *to intervene at a level no deeper than that at which the energy and resources of the client can be committed to problem solving and to change.*

I have analyzed the tendency for increases in individual autonomy in organizations to push the appropriate level of intervention deeper when the first criterion is followed. Opposed to this is the countervailing influence of the second criterion to work closer to the surface in order to enlist the energy and support of organization members in the change process. Arguments have been presented for resolving this dilemma in favor of the second, more conservative, criterion. The dilemma remains, of course; the continuing tension under which the change agent works is between the desire to lead and push, or to collaborate and follow. The middle ground is never very stable, and I suspect we show our values and preferences by which criterion we choose to maximize when we are under the stress of difficult and ambiguous client-consultant relationships.

References

Byrd, R.E. "Training in a Nongroup." *Journal of Humanistic Psychology,* 7 no. 1, (1967): pp. 18-27.

Clark, J.V. "Task Group Therapy." Unpublished manuscript, University of California, Los Angeles, 1966.

6. Strategic Pay and High-Involvement Organizations: Interview With Edward Lawler

Conrad N. Jackson

Edward E. Lawler, III, has served on the faculties of Yale, Michigan, and USC. He has authored prolific academic and practitioner publications on motivation, compensation, and high-involvement management practices. In 1985 he was named one of the Top Ten Organization Development Consultants by Training and Development Journal. *He currently is director of the Center for Effective Organizations, Graduate School of Business Administration, University of Southern California, Los Angeles, CA 90089-1421.*

Jackson: Your work on designing compensation systems that motivate workers is especially well-known and timely. I thought *Pay and Organization Development* was an extremely useful and insightful book, and I know you've done a lot of research and consulting on this topic since then. Could we begin by getting some of your current thinking about this issue?

Lawler: I have just published my third major book on compensation, called *Strategic Pay.* In a sense, it is much more organizational than the other two. The first one, *Pay and Organizational Effectiveness* (1971), looked at theory and research on the effects of pay systems on individual behavior. The second one, *Pay and Organization Development* (1981), was much more action-oriented, and dealt with pay practices in organizations. *Strategic Pay* starts with the organization's strategy and structure, and then specifies how you create a reward system which supports it. It is rather prescriptive from an organizational context. For example, I say organizations that want employee involvement need to pay for skills, use gainsharing and profit sharing, and develop employee financial ownership programs.

In a sense it goes back to the issue I started with when I first went to graduate school: Why do some people behave more effectively and work harder in organizations than others? And the two streams which I am primarily involved in today—how to motivate people with pay and effectively use employee involvement—are 30-year manifestations of that original question. I am intrigued with reward systems because I think

---

Conrad Jackson, Ph.D., is Associate Professor of Management at the University of Alabama in Huntsville, Huntsville, AL 35899.

they have a tremendous impact on why people do what they do in the workplace. I am also intrigued with employee involvement and participative management because I think how decisions are made and how power is allocated are very critical influences on what motivates individuals. A lot of my recent writing has been on the convergence of those two; that is, what kind of reward systems support getting people more involved in the business, understanding the business, and learning more about the business.

I got disenchanted with pay research in the late '60s because most of the pay practices that made sense to me, like pay for skills and being more open about pay practices, weren't being used by most organizations. I have been recharged in the area of compensation through the last ten years because, all of a sudden, the floodgates seem to have opened, and organizations are much more willing to experiment in the area of pay.

Jackson: It seems like they're trying to get more for their money.

Lawler: Basically they recognize their old systems are broken, and they are looking at pay as a place to gain competitive advantage. They are saying, in essence, that they're spending all these dollars—maybe they can spend them smarter. Or, as was the case with the General Foods experiment in Topeka, they come up with new organization designs that are more participative and have more employee involvement. This causes their pay practices to be highly discrepant with the other ways they are operating. So a lot of the work I now do in pay is because somebody calls me and says, "We've done this and this, and all of a sudden our pay system looks broken. Fix it."

Jackson: Would it be fair to say that you are a strong advocate of tying pay to performance?

Lawler: Yes, but I think I have made a major change over the years. I have been studying it largely because of my interests in employee involvement and organization design. Right from the beginning, I was an advocate of pay for performance because of all the psychological research that shows it can be a powerful motivator. Despite what you read in various popular press pieces or in some psychological theories, there is overwhelming evidence that pay can be a very strong driver of performance.

Part of my original work looked at how you can tie individual pay to individual performance, and what the consequences are. As I get more into organization design and employee involvement, I am increasingly recommending that pay for performance be focused at the plant, group, or total organization level. I am intrigued with the question of how to create motivating pay systems that reward groups or plants. In many cases, individual pay for performance simply doesn't fit the work design or the management style of the organization. In fact, to continue to try to create individual pay for performance plans in some organizations is counterproductive. This is particularly true where work is highly interdependent and, as a result, teamwork is needed. So I continue to be interested in tying pay to performance, and I still recommend it in many cases. But I know that the type of pay for performance plan which is appropriate for the organization depends on the organization's design characteristics and management style. These are the kinds of issues I've dealt with in *Strategic Pay.*

Jackson: So if I understand correctly, you are recommending a move toward compensating groups rather than individuals?

Lawler: Often I say, "Let's pay the individual for skills, and let's pay for performance when and where we can measure it and capture the key interdependencies." Let's say you have a chemical plant, for instance. There you need to pay for performance at the plant level because cooperation is critical, and performance is best measured at the plant level. In environments where you're trying to create work teams, create participative structures, and shared accountability and responsibility, you have to reward performance at the group or even larger level.

Jackson: Then would that tend to make performance appraisal less important?

Lawler: It certainly ought to change them. I have recently published a book, *Designing Performance Appraisal Systems,* which deals with this issue. It argues that performance appraisal still may be needed to determine what kind of skill-based pay increase somebody will get. For example, if someone masters a new computer language, this needs to be recognized and determined and rewarded. Performance appraisals may address performance, but they often are not tied to an actual pay change. I think performance appraisal is undergoing a slow but sure change. It is becoming both more participative and more broadly based. The old one-over-one approach, where supervisors evaluate subordinates, simply doesn't fit the realities of the modern organization. In many situations peer appraisals, subordinate, and/or group appraisals make more sense.

Jackson: Do you find that certain parts of the country or certain industries more readily accept involvement and newer compensation or performance appraisal ideas?

Lawler: I'm not sure that there is a regional difference. But I think it is much easier to do in new organizations because they don't have the old habits and practices to unlearn. I also think there is some truth to the view that organizations are more likely to do new things when they're hurting and not performing particularly well. So a lot of our work in the last decade has been in manufacturing organizations that are facing tough international competition. They have reached the conclusion that simply doing the old better is not good enough, so they are willing to do very different things to be competitive.

Jackson: Let me ask you to think like a consultant for a minute. Do you use the term "OD" to describe your expertise or your work with clients? Or do you find that the term is no longer useful?

Lawler: I use it occasionally. I am more likely to say that I am interested in organizational change, reward systems, and employee involvement when asked to state my interests. My concern about using the term organization development may go back to the way I first started to view OD when I was at Yale in the mid-60s. OD meant T-groups, interpersonal process training, and group facilitation. In corporations, people who call themselves organization development professionals often still concentrate on group process issues and training issues. I don't think I have particular expertise in these areas, so I tend to be very cautious in using the term. Incidentally, I do see people increasingly using the term "organizational effectiveness" to describe what used to be OD activities. Not surprisingly, I think the most effective organization development consultants I have seen are those that can do more than group process facilitation and training. They are able to think of complex multi-system interventions.

Jackson: How do you explain your role to a client? As a consultant, what are you supposed to do, and what are they supposed to do? What is the contract?

Lawler: It varies depending on whether they are involved in a research project or whether I'm simply in there as an individual doing consulting work. My contracts vary all the way from, "I'm just here for a day to give you some ideas about some changes that you might develop" through, "We're going to be in a three- to four-year relationship, where I will give you ideas that support a major change effort. Then together we will assess, evaluate, and alter it if that is needed."

As I have gotten more senior in my career, I have spent less intensive time in organizations, and I find myself less able to spend two or three years working regularly with an organization on a particular project or a particular effort.

I should add that I'm not the type of person who goes into an organization and gathers data, goes away for three weeks, and then comes back with a new skill-based pay plan, gainsharing plan, or employee involvement strategy. I believe in a joint development process for any intervention or change. So I almost always ask for a task force or a diagonal-slice committee to work with, and act as a facilitator and developer with them.

Jackson: And you become a resource to them, allowing them to pick your brain?

Lawler: Yes. And that is true of all the projects that we do through the center [The Center for Effective Organizations]. We always position them as joint efforts in which we will help the organization facilitate their changes, acting as resources to them. Ultimately we are trying to transfer the knowledge we have to the organization, and make it able to design change and learn from change.

Jackson: Can you identify any factors which seem to make some consultation experiences more or less successful than others?

Lawler: A large number of factors! However, I am constantly amazed at how poor I am at predicting which one is going to turn into a good consulting effort. Sometimes when I think there is no way anything meaningful can happen, it turns out to be a great project! Because of this, I am often willing to take on projects that appear to have a low probability of success. My experience is that so much changes in a long-term project that good ones can become bad ones and vice versa. The changes can include a change in senior management, a dramatic financial change, a takeover or buyout. All sorts of external events can intervene which change the fundamental nature of a project.

Jackson: Among the things that change, it seems to me, is the stream of management ideas that people are being bombarded by. What can managers do to try to make sense of it all? Do you see any underlying principles, trends, or ideas that help make sense out of this chaos?

Lawler: Yes, I believe there are some underlying principles that one ought to keep in mind. When new practices or technologies come along, I am intrigued by them. I admire people who develop new management practices. What we need to do is become intelligent consumers. We have to ask the right questions about what they are changing in an organization, and what impact these are likely to have on an organization's effectiveness and on its quality of work life.

Currently, for example, there is a national interest in total quality programs. The same issues are involved as in any major organizational change program. I think you have to ask, "What does it do to the reward system?", "What does it do to the information systems?", "What does it do to the power distribution?", and "What does it do to the kind of skill level and knowledge level of people?" Once you have some feeling for these factors, you need to ask whether the changes are ones that are likely to have a positive impact on effectiveness because people will be more motivated, more committed, more knowledgeable, and more useful to the organization. And, of course, what will it do to the people? Will it make them be more satisfied, and make their lives better?

Jackson: Would the title of your recent book *High Involvement Management* imply that you think that is where we're going?

Lawler: I don't think we are going there for all kinds of products and services. We have one very well-developed paradigm of management— the traditional top-down bureaucratic model—and have seen that it works OK in some situations, and not so well in the others. What I think we have been chipping away at since the '40s or '50s is an alternative model that calls for a different distribution of power, knowledge, information, and rewards. Slowly but surely it is becoming a developed piece of technology.

I don't think it is anywhere near as developed as the traditional model is, but we are getting a better and better understanding of what it looks like and how it can be operated effectively. The more I see companies implement it, the more I realize just how fundamentally different organizations have to be if they are going to operate with a true commitment to employee involvement. They don't just have to train their supervisors to listen or hold great meetings. They have to change just about every feature of the way they operate as organizations.

Likert, Argyris, McGregor, and others who wrote in the '50s and before gave us some interesting concepts, but they didn't give us much technology. What is fun today is to try to develop technology that helps those ideas become reality. I think that for a lot of organizations, it is the way they have to go. In other words, they have to develop management systems which better utilize the people who work for them. If they don't, they aren't going to be competitive in today's business environment.

The simple fact is that in the United States, we have a high wage level. If employees don't add a lot of value to the products or services their organizations offer, they [the organizations] are not going to be competitive with many other countries. The basic problem with the bureaucratic model is that it asks too little of most employees. It doesn't give them a chance to add enough value to the product to justify their wages.

Jackson: Where does the involvement approach fit?

Lawler: You need products or services that create relatively complex work for the high involvement model to make the most sense. And of course you need people who enjoy that kind of work.

There are a lot of examples of repetitive work that are hard to make interesting and challenging and, as a result, you cannot rely on the intrinsic interest of the work as the source of motivation and control in the workplace. A lot of low-level service jobs are obviously of that nature. A lot of manufacturing work is of that nature. Many of those jobs already have left the country. In the service sector, many can't leave because they have to be delivered in person. For example, fast food restaurants have to keep their jobs as do gas stations and toll roads.

Jackson: You know, it's scary to think there are jobs out there that have built-in alienation, but because they have to be done, somebody has to do them. Who decides who is going to get that work?

Lawler: It is scary. It is a continuing problem that we have work that isn't the kind of work that mature healthy human beings should be doing. Of course, it is not unique to our society. All societies have that kind of work. There are some people who have low needs for growth, so that is all they want to do or can do. This partially solves the problem. We can also export that work to low-wage countries and poorly-developed countries that have large numbers of people who are willing to do that work even if its not very psychologically satisfying. Some of that work is ultimately subject to automation, and will increasingly disappear. For example, look at how the number of employees in gas stations has dropped.

Influences on a Career Path

Jackson: Your career has developed as the field of OD has unfolded. Did you think of yourself as an OD person from the beginning, or as a psychologist?

Lawler: I started my academic career as a psychologist. I was an undergraduate psychology major, and my Ph.D. is in psychology (1964). When I went to Berkeley to get my Ph.D., I didn't even know what the field of industrial psychology was all about. I took one undergraduate course in industrial psychology. So when I went to graduate school, I was searching for a field and a fit. I knew I was interested in organizations and how they operated, with a particular interest in issues of motivation and satisfaction. I quickly discovered that industrial psychology was concerned with individual differences—selection and placement—while my interests were organization design, motivation, and satisfaction.

About that time people were starting to talk about organizational psychology and distinguishing it from industrial psychology. I quickly identified with the organizational psychology area. All through graduate school I never thought of organization development as a field. In fact I am not sure anybody did at that time. The major activity that was going on was the work on T-groups and encounter sessions.

Jackson: What sort of stamp did Berkeley put on you, then?

Lawler: Three key people—Ed Ghiselli, Mason Haire, and Lyman Porter—put very much of a research stamp with a fairly heavy theory bent. Ghiselli was a more traditional industrial psychologist, so he was probably least impactful. Mason Haire and Porter were early creators of the organizational psychology paradigm—particularly Mason Haire. So from them I got a strong interest in empirical data and in studying the phenomena of organizing and how organizations impact on people.

Porter was into his research on satisfaction and the relationship between characteristics of organizations and the satisfaction of members. That was very interesting to me throughout my graduate program. I came out of the program with a psychology orientation and a research orientation. Action and change were not very important to me. I had no skills as a consultant. I was very suspicious of research that involved action, and very wary of getting involved in things which would look too applied and too action-oriented.

Jackson: And yet you ended up at Yale, where they were thinking about action a lot.

Lawler: Yes, they were. They hired me to broaden their program.

Jackson: You were the anchor on the other end?

Lawler: I was the anchor on the other end. As soon as I got there, I ended up joking with the existing group about being different from them and how my interests were very much more scientific than theirs. I'm particularly talking about Chris Argyris, who was the dominant figure there at the time; Roger Harrison, who was very active in NTL; and Fritz Steel, who arrived at about the same time and identified with Argyris and Roger Harrison. They formed quite an impressive group.

Jackson: There were a lot of remarkable people on that faculty in that era. I don't know if you intersected with all of them.

Lawler: I did with a number of them. Fairly quickly after I arrived, we hired Tim Hall, Ben Schneider, and Richard Hackman. Many of them were more like me in interests and proved to be incredibly good colleagues. Clay Alderfer was a graduate student and later a faculty member. Roy Lewicki was a faculty member. So there was quite an array of impressive faculty and graduate students—Greg Oldham, Martin Evans, John Wanous, Corty Cammann, and Lee Bolman.

Argyris provided a very powerful model of tolerance for other people's ideas and debate of ideas. He encouraged people to do things other than the kinds of things he was interested in. So there was no dominant research model there that you had to follow, nor a dominant conceptual model. There was constantly a tension between what's good research, what's good theory, and what's good practice.

Certainly a lot of my interest in practice was stimulated by Chris constantly asking questions about practice and the application of research. The time I spent at Yale was incredibly important in my thinking and development, because it forced me to examine the kind of research and value paradigm I brought with me from Berkeley and modify it in some important ways.

Chris got me into the field to do more than just hand out questionnaires. He helped me to see how practice can inform theory and research; how, indeed, if you produce change in organizations, you can often learn more about a phenomena than if you just study it passively through questionnaires and interviews. Clearly in looking at my career, the Berkeley threesome of Haire, Ghiselli, and Porter were very important— particularly Porter. And then during my years at Yale, Argyris was an extremely powerful influence. While I was at Yale, I formed very important working alliances with Hackman, Tim Hall, and some of the others. But Argyris was the most powerful thought leader at the time.

Jackson: I believe it was about this time that you and Lyman Porter were collaborating, too, on what we now know as the Porter-Lawler Model. (See Figure 1 on the following page.)

Lawler: Yes, it came out of my dissertation and was written up in 1968 as a book which we co-authored. I spent a lot of my first two or three years at Yale working on completing the research agenda that I had begun in graduate school. Porter brought to that thinking his pioneering work on satisfaction and the determinants of satisfaction. My interest was in motivation and the relationship of satisfaction to motivation. That model was a product of our discussions and writing together, and then I continued to do research on it at Yale.

My work with Hackman on job design was a chance to apply my thinking about motivation to work design. Hackman had a strong interest

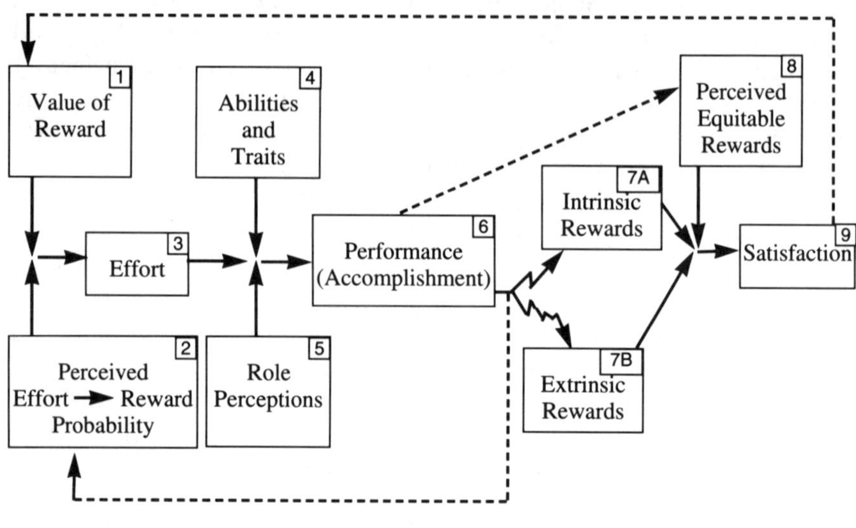

in characteristics of tasks, and I in motivation theory. So the combination led to our writing about job design and its effects on motivation and satisfaction.

Jackson: What provided the seeds for the compensation work you have done ever since?

Lawler: My compensation work actually preceded the job design work. When I was in graduate school, Mason Haire, who knew the literature a heck of a lot better than I did, pointed out that there was very little research on compensation as a determinant of behavior. I dove into the literature on motivation and money and found only a few things. Probably the most influential book was one by William Whyte called *Money and Motivation,* written in 1955. I was very intrigued by the issues raised in it and put a number of questions about compensation into my dissertation data collection.

I decided to concentrate on compensation during my first few years of doing empirical research. In many respects, it seemed like compensation was a good place to start because it was an important issue, it was under-researched, and it was probably easier to conceptualize and quantify than something like work design. When Hackman joined the Yale faculty, that was my opportunity to study motivation that wasn't based on financial or extrinsic rewards.

Jackson: That is the little fork in the middle of that model that recognizes intrinsic and extrinsic rewards?

Lawler: Yes, I was already thinking about that before the work with Hackman. But the work with him allowed me to operationalize and test some of my thinking. Still, at this time in the late '60s and early '70s, I wasn't particularly into thinking about applications in organizations. That really followed from my later years at Yale and my initial years at the University of Michigan, which was the next stop in my career.

Jackson: That model also incorporates the individual's perception of equity. Where did that idea come from?

Lawler: That tied into my interest in compensation. I was challenged by the work that Adams was doing on equity theory, and curious as to how it related to the work that Porter had already done in his studies of job satisfaction. The Adams model argued that feelings of equity were strong motivators of performance. My initial guess was that he was wrong. That led me to do the only series of laboratory studies that I have done in my career. Most of those were targeted at challenging elements of the Adams model. I was intrigued because my model argued that performance causes satisfaction, while his argument was more that satisfaction or feelings of equity, as he called them, would cause performance.

Jackson: That has turned out to be an important lesson for managers, too.

Lawler: When I first started my work, it was accepted that satisfaction was an important determinant of performance. Operationally, that meant that all you had to do was go around and keep people satisfied and happy and somehow the organization would be effective. That has turned out to be not only simplistic, but incorrect.

It was the convergence of these ideas that raised questions of overall organization design and policy for me. How could you design an organization that would simultaneously motivate people and satisfy them? That seemed to be an enormous challenge and an intellectually interesting issue.

I think it's fair to say that while I was at Yale, I was much more focused at the individual level than at the organization level. I had a complex map of what an individual was like, but not a very rich map of what an organization was like. Organization characteristics were largely seen as independent variables which predicted how individuals would react.

Jackson: Had you begun to do consulting by this time?

Lawler: I didn't do much consulting until my last few years at Yale. There were two reasons for that. First, I didn't have any skills. And second, I thought that it was sure death in terms of academic survival. I felt I would never make it in research if I spent very much time consulting. So it was an easy choice for me to make. Nobody asked me, and I didn't feel particularly motivated to do it. Although, I was always very curious about consulting. Again, Chris Argyris provided a model of somebody who was successfully writing and consulting. I was always intrigued with how he balanced them and what kind of consulting he did. He was a very important role model because prior to him, the leading academics were pretty much strictly publishers and teachers. When they consulted, they gave a speech. They didn't change an organization; they weren't action-oriented.

Jackson: So about 1972 you moved on to the University of Michigan. What pulled you there?

Lawler: It was an interesting move. I had long had an approach/avoidance reaction to Michigan. I admired many of the people who were there and the sort of research that they did. I was intrigued by both their large-scale research projects and their ability to do evaluation and field research. I should also confess that I was not particularly dedicated to being in the classroom. There I had the chance to take an appointment which was primarily in the Institute for Social Research with a joint appointment in psychology. With the appointment in psychology I could just work with Ph.D. students if that was all I wanted to do. It looked like a good mix for me.

The situation at Yale at that time was troubled. Although I had received an early promotion to Associate Professor, several years later my promotion to tenure was delayed at the university level. At Michigan I jumped into a thriving group of organizational researchers. Stan Seashore and Bob Kahn were key figures. Likert's influence was still there, too, but he was retired.

Moving there gave me the chance to do two things that I had never done before. One was raise research money. In fact, it was more than just a chance. It was basically, "If you are interested in a job at the Institute of Social Research, you have to be self-supporting." So I had to learn how to get grant money from foundations, the federal government, and others. The other thing it allowed me to do was large-scale research projects. Most of the research I did there was evaluation research.

Jackson: What did you evaluate?

Lawler: Our single biggest effort, lasting almost ten years, involved the creation and evaluation of a number of labor management organization development projects. We got money—several million dollars—to create and evaluate demonstration projects that would establish the validity of and describe the various forms of labor management cooperation. They started in the early '70s and continued into the '80s. They resulted in a series of books. I edited two on organizational assessment and organizational change, and other books were on specific projects. In fact, just recently yet another book out of that research stream was published by Mike Mock of Michigan State.

Jackson: Any chance that this is how you got tied to General Foods' Topeka pet food plant?

Lawler: The Topeka plant effort was a part of that stream. The labor management cooperation projects were large-scale action research efforts because we needed to generate change. To do that we created a Washington office that handled the change piece of it, and then we launched the development of measurement instruments. While all that was going on, I continued to be interested in pay system work. That is how I got involved with Topeka. I was interested in pay and employee involvement. The company was interested in pay systems and its approaches to participation. So I went in to help study its system's effectiveness and, in particular, look at alternative approaches to compensation that would fit the management style.

Jackson: Who was your connection to that? Were you connected to Dick Walton?

Lawler: No. It was the plant manager there, Ed Dulworth. I worked with him and ultimately joined a General Foods corporate task force that was set up to evaluate the effectiveness of the Topeka plant. Doug Jenkins and I did an attitude survey there, and we compared the results with data from other settings. We found extremely positive attitudes. General Foods did some internal economic analysis which showed the same thing. However, before the work reached fruition, the key management team at the plant was asked to leave.

My work at Topeka was very influential on me. It showed me two things. The first was the importance of system-wide design if you are committed to employee involvement and participation. Remember, I was at the University of Michigan, and the Michigan research on employee participation tended to focus on leadership style and managerial behavior. Topeka helped me to understand that there are a lot of systems in an organization that you have to rethink if you want to operate with a participative, high-involvement approach to management.

The second learning involved how much flexibility you have when you start a new organization. In fact, another one of our evaluation research projects, which was the study of the startup of a new pharmaceutical plant in North Carolina, came out of that Topeka work. Dennis Perkins, Ronnie Nieva, and I did an intensive three-year observation study.

Jackson: Was the pay for knowledge concept at Topeka when you got there?

Lawler: Yes. To the best of my knowledge, they got the idea from their contacts in Scandinavia and at Proctor and Gamble. I almost immediately became enamored with the concept and have continued to pursue it to this day. All of a sudden, it seems to have caught on and become extremely popular.

Jackson: Another thing that was going on while you were at Michigan was your interest in and writing about the quality of work life. How did that get introduced into your career?

Lawler: I think part of it was going to Michigan. They already had the Quality of Employment Survey that they did on a regular basis to look at the national workplace. I became interested in how to design organizations that treated employees as stakeholders. I started working with some accountants, looking at issues of human asset accounting and those measurement technologies. I got rather swept up in the idea that organizations should be held accountable in the public arena for how they treat their employees.

Phil Mirvis and I helped one company, Graphic Controls—a small publicly traded company in Buffalo—issue an annual quality of work life report as a section of their financial annual report. In the '70s I thought we might be moving toward companies issuing annual reports that looked at how they treated their employees. At one point, I was on a Department of Commerce committee that was looking into how to do it, what kind of standards to set, and whether organizations could in fact systematically report on those issues.

As we entered the late '70s and early '80s, people became more concerned about productivity and international competitiveness. The humanism of the '70s faded into the background, and that idea lost momentum.

Jackson: You mentioned that while you were at Michigan, your own thinking began to move from an individual focus more toward larger-system focus.

Lawler: I think that happened because of the kind of work I was doing at Michigan. Evaluation research put me into the field a lot. I spent most of my time in organizations watching somebody act as a change agent or acting as a change agent myself. Watching change happen, I got a lot more comfortable with and had to give a lot more thought to organizations and how they operate, what made them accept or reject change, and why we could or couldn't get a project going in an organization. Of course that combined with the fact that with people like Seashore, Likert, Kahn, and Katz at Michigan there was a strong organization theory bent. Finally, I ended up with an incredibly good group of doctoral students— Dave Nadler, Doug Jenkins, Nina Gupta, Jack Drexler, Dennis Perkins, Dave Berg, Mark Fitchman, and Phil Mirvis—who were there with me, and they helped me learn something about organization development and organizational theory.

Jackson: So it was about 1978 that you headed out to USC?

Lawler: Yes. That was a tough decision because I had a good stay at Michigan. I learned a lot, and I had a lot of interesting research going on. In fact I didn't just leave Michigan. I eased out of Michigan for several years because I had many projects going that I didn't want to just leave.

Two things were critical in my leaving. One was the personal issue of marrying somebody who wanted to live in Southern California, and the other was the fund-raising feature of the ISR system. I had to raise substantial amounts of money every year to keep the research unit that I had built up alive and well. As I looked at the economic situation, it just didn't look favorable for continuing support. There was an emerging negative attitude in Washington toward social science research. I got very concerned about whether I could continue to bring in the money that was needed to keep what was then a fairly large research activity alive.

I decided to move to the University of Southern California's business school. It was the first time that I had ever been in a business school. After a relatively short period of time, I decided that I enjoyed running a research center and that the challenge was to start one at USC. That is when I got support from the business school to start The Center for Effective Organizations.

The Center for Effective Organizations
Jackson: Your principle organizational affiliation now is with The Center for Effective Organizations at USC. Can you describe the center's work?

Lawler: In many ways the center is based on the experiences that I had at Michigan, but it differs in two major respects. First, it is more involved in action and change. The Michigan unit was an evaluation research unit. The Center for Effective Organizations is an action research unit. The distinction is that we are jointly responsible for making things happen and for assessing what happens. The second important difference is that the unit at USC tends to rely on private-sector funding—company money— for most of its support.

One of the things that differentiates our center from most business school centers is that we hire full-time researchers into the center. I learned the importance of this at Michigan, where we hired a number of very good people into ISR and, in essence, made them responsible for creating a research program and managing research projects.

My experience is that it is very hard to do field research if you have teaching responsibilities. Over the ten-plus years that the center has been operating, we have been fortunate to be able to hire a number of outstanding researchers who are full-time in the center—Jay Galbraith, Gerry Ledford, Susan Cohen, Monty Mohrman, and Susan Mohrman. They have to be able to balance writing with dealing on an ongoing basis with companies. It is not an easy role, and it is difficult to find people who are simultaneously good at action and good at writing up research.

Jackson: Are the companies who support you essentially consulting clients, or do they simply support you as benefactors?

Lawler: It is a combination of the two. We have over 40 companies that give us an annual contribution to support our general operations. And at any point in time, we have active research projects going with 10 to 20 companies.

Jackson: What kind of projects does your center get involved with?

Lawler: There are two kinds. The first are ones where organizations come to us and say they are considering some change or some innovation and want our help in installing and assessing it. These projects have involved opening new plants, putting in new information systems, implementing skill-based pay systems and gainsharing plans, and other new organizational practices. We look at each as an opportunity to study that practice and, at the same time, learn something about organizations.

The second kind of project uses a multi-company approach. We go to a number of companies that agree to participate and bear the cost of it. The largest multi-company study that we have done is a study of employee involvement in the Fortune 1000. Three years ago we did the initial questionnaire survey to see what new practices they were adopting in the employee involvement area, and wrote the results in a monograph. We are now completing a second round of questionnaires, so we can see what has changed.

Jackson: If somebody comes to you and says, "We want to implement such and such program," do you question their diagnosis—whether or not they've correctly ferreted out the problem and have the appropriate solution in mind?

Lawler: The first thing we have to decide is whether it is something we can even do through the center. Anything we do through the center has to be in the public domain. They have to be willing to allow us to write it up, and we have to be allowed to collect data. In addition, we have to feel that it is a significant enough activity to warrant attention.

Our normal first step is to do a diagnosis to see if in fact the idea they have is one that makes any sense. Often, organizations will come to us and say, "We want skill-based pay, or we want gainsharing." But after some investigation we sometimes have to say, "It would be a great research project, but we can't see that it is the right thing for you to do." So we end up with a number of dry holes in our research model.

If you are in an action research mode as contrasted with an evaluation research mode, I think you have a different responsibility for telling organizations that they shouldn't proceed with something because the probability of success is relatively low. If you are in a pure evaluation research mode, the fact that the effort is unlikely to succeed is really irrelevant. You are supposed to sit there and study it. In fact, a failure can be as informative as a success.

Jackson: It sounds like the work of the center keeps you quite busy. Do you ever look ahead and say, "Here's where I want to go with my career?" Are there some things you have charted for yourself but haven't achieved yet?

Lawler: I don't tend to think too far ahead as far as my career directions go. I wanted to get a reputation for being able to do strong empirical research, and I was able to do a lot of that early in my career. I did want to get more action-oriented, both because I find that interesting and because I think you learn more from that in many cases. I wanted to get more into institution building. I was able to do that at Michigan and now at USC with The Center for Effective Organizations.

Now I am most intrigued with continuing to develop my ideas around employee involvement. I would like to see those ideas evolve into a widely implemented set of practices. I am a long way from having convinced a lot of organizations which should adopt them that in fact they should adopt them. As a result, the adoption rate is a lot lower than I'd like to see it.

Many of my ideas are still only partially developed. My undone tasks, at this point, are basically changing how American businesses are managed, particularly concerning issues of involvement and compensation. Although we don't know everything about either one of those, there is a lot less utilization of the new ideas than there should be. So I would like to both develop the ideas, and see them more widely adopted.

Jackson: I have seen some other successful OD people who have reached that point in their careers. The next step—spreading adoption—is change on an industry or even national scale.

Lawler: Yes, and in a sense The Center for Effective Organizations is set up to facilitate national change. We have over 40 companies supporting us, and they are a vehicle for us to influence change. We do projects through them, which changes them. They are role models for a lot of other companies. So we hope that by working through them, it will ultimately change more than just them.

Jackson: Is there anything really obvious that we have missed here that we should have talked about? Anything else on your mind now that we should include?

Lawler: Overall I tend to think of my career as having four stages which are marked by job moves: graduate school at Berkeley and jobs at Yale, Michigan, and USC. One of the things that strikes me about all four places is how incredibly lucky I have been. Everywhere I have been, I have had great colleagues. I don't think that was great planning on my part, or great recruiting on my part once I got there. I attribute it more to luck or coincidence than anything else.

As I think about my research career, I realize just how strongly I have been influenced by the people I have worked with. I learn a lot from listening to others and from conversation. I am more comfortable with that than with sitting in a room by myself reading or writing. And I can easily see myself as having gone in very different directions if it hadn't been for the kind of social situations that I ended up in at the four major stops in my career.

I sit back and think about the talent that I have been and am surrounded with, and I am amazed and thankful. The three people I worked with at Berkeley were all nationally-known leaders. The Yale group was really exceptional. The Michigan group was great, and had a great history. When I came to USC, there were a number of good people, and I have had good luck with hiring outstanding people into the center. If you look at my vitae, you see a lot of co-authored things. Part of the way I have remained current and been productive is to be with people who are really talented. In a sense I have ridden along with them.

Jackson: That's interesting. Perhaps part of the paradigm of participative management or high-involvement management is having lots of good people around to work and interact with so that their thoughts and values can stimulate one another.

Lawler: Yes. I am sure that if my first couple of jobs had been at places where there wasn't much research going on, I would have ended up going in a very different career direction.

Part Three: Examples of Interventions in Industry

7. Socio-Technical Redesign of an HR Division

Joseph S. Fiorelli and Mark Kizilos

This case study describes the redesign of the socio-technical systems (STS) of a Human Resources (HR) division within a Fortune 30 manufacturing company. A model which can facilitate the application of non-linear STS redesigns in other corporate staff functions is also discussed.

Organizational Setting

The organizational setting is a global division of a 12 billion-dollar diversified corporation. The division has over 3,200 employees worldwide with about half of this number in its West Coast division headquarters. The division had just come off a record year in terms of both sales and profits. But by the beginning of the third quarter in 1989, it was clear that the division would have to significantly reduce spending and downsize to match its current business performance. Staffed to meet rising demand for an ambitious growth curve, the division was now oversized. After a series of difficult layoffs, plant shut downs to burn off excess inventory, and spending cuts, the division shrank from 3,200 to 2,700 employees.

The division Human Resources function was hit hard by the business downturn. Approximately 20 percent of the department's employees were laid off (8 of 40), and spending was cut back substantially. Combined, the budget and personnel cuts resulted in a 40 percent reduction in the HR department's resources.

Becoming Customer-Focused: New Vision for HR

The project sponsor, the HR director, wanted the HR department to become more customer-focused. The department had become demoralized by the staff and budget cuts, and many of the remaining employees were overworked. As a result, HR services were slow or nonexistent and the division's credibility was suffering. The director wanted to put the HR function back on track. With the assistance of the Organization Development (OD) manager, he announced that an OD intervention was being planned to facilitate a redesign of the department. By using an STS approach (Cummings, 1976; Emery and Trist, 1960; Hanna, 1988; Pasmore, 1988; Sherwood, 1988), it was hoped that department activities could be streamlined and resources re-dedicated to provide a more value-added, strategic HR service.

Joseph Fiorelli, Ph.D., is an organizational consultant for Ernst & Young, 3200 Park Center Drive, Ste. 900, Costa Mesa, CA 92606. Mark Kizilos is a doctoral student in the Department of Management and Organization, 305 Bridge Hall, the University of Southern California, Los Angeles, CA 90089.

Staffing the Redesign Project

A graduate intern in Organizational Behavior was recruited in 1989 to serve as the project leader for the redesign effort. This person reported to the OD manager, who served as a *shadow consultant* for the project. The project leader became a full-time member of the HR function for the duration of his ten-month assignment.

When the project leader arrived, he was full of enthusiasm and energy. His initial introduction to the organization, however, was somewhat demoralizing:

> I took this job to "get my hands dirty" on a real STS redesign project. I figured everyone would be as enthusiastic about the redesign as I was. But the week before I started, a number of people had been laid off. In fact, my office was vacant due to a layoff a few days earlier. This made it hard to build trust and interest in the redesign. Things were made worse when, at the end of my first week, a plant shutdown was announced. I started to realize the attitudes in the department were going to be a major obstacle to the redesign process.

Six people initially were selected as members of the redesign team, but one chose not to participate. The reasons for declining membership were revealed in a conversation with the project leader:

> It wasn't anything against you or the project. It's just that I don't have the time to be involved in some big task team project. Besides, I have seen what happens with these task teams. They spend a lot of time and energy developing plans to improve things, and then make a big presentation. But that is all—nothing changes.

The final team membership consisted of two Employee Relations specialists, one recruiter, one Staffing secretary, and one Benefits manager.

Getting the Project Under Way

Prior to the redesign team's first meeting, the project leader conducted interviews with each HR manager and the HR director. The purpose of these interviews was to develop a mission and objectives for the redesign team that would be acceptable to the project sponsor and the Management Steering Committee (the HR management staff). Constraints, or "givens," for the project were also determined in these interviews. Three project "givens" were as follows.

■ No additional headcount could be added in the redesign.

■ The redesign was to require limited financial investment.

■ The redesign would support the introduction of a new role within the HR function—the Human Resources Consultant (HRC).

The HRC role was to be based on a similar role that the OD manager had experienced during his previous work at Corning, Inc. He described the HRC role as:

> an attempt to position the HR division as a meaningful contributor to the business by aligning key, high-talent HR professionals with the business's line functions. The HRCs are expected to attend their clients' staff meetings and build rapport and

trust within their client organizations. Eventually, the HRCs will be in a position to provide HR insights to their clients on key business issues in a real-time, strategic manner.

The interviews resulted in the following Team Mission and Objectives.

HR Redesign Team Mission

"Conduct an analysis of the work and people processes in HR to identify improvement opportunities and develop recommendations for the main body of HR in support of the HRC concept."

HR Redesign Team Objectives

■ Develop a basic understanding of the department's work flow, including inputs, transformation processes, and outputs.

■ See the relationship between HR units and customers.

■ Identify redundant/outdated processes.

■ Improve the balance of the work system.

■ Improve HR teamwork and cooperation.

■ Develop a vision of what the future HR main body should look like.

■ Streamline policies and procedures where possible.

■ Develop a plan with recommendations for quality/productivity improvement (i.e., redesign the work system to better achieve the organization mission).

■ Present the redesign plan to the HR Management Steering Committee.

Once the project givens were clear and approved by the Management Steering Committee, the stage was set to hold the redesign team's first meeting. The first meeting focused on educating the team members in the principles of socio-technical systems. This session was conducted by the OD manager. The HR director presented the team with its mission, objectives, and constraints. In addition, the project leader presented basic concepts on group interaction and facilitated a brainstorming exercise on team expectations as a team building activity. Reflecting back on that first meeting, the project leader observed:

There is a lot of education needed in order to get the redesign team up and running. The problem I faced, however, was that people started to see the project as too academic. They thought that it was just an academic exercise to give an intern some work to keep busy. It was difficult overcoming these initial feelings. These attitudes almost sunk the project at several points.

STS Redesign

The redesign followed the ten-step process shown in Figure 1.

Figure 1: Major Steps in the Redesign Process

1. Contracting, Goal Setting & Strategy Affirmation
2. Project Rollout & Redesign Team Selection
3. Redesign Team Training
4. Environmental Scan/Customer Feedback
5. Macro Work Flow Analysis
6. Micro Work Flow Analysis
7. Redesign to Control Variances and Meet Change Goals
8. Presentation of Redesign Proposal
9. Management Steering Committee Approval and Implementation
10. Evaluation and Self-Renewal

After the initial goal setting and start-up training sessions, the first team task assigned was to better understand what services the HR department currently provided. Initially, the team put together a rough macro-level map of these services. This map was then expanded by each team member interviewing five others in the department to determine what major functions they performed. The interview results yielded a greater understanding of the *micro*-level detail behind each of the department's major services. The details that filled ten flipchart pages were discussed by the team members, and the charts were condensed to elimininate all redundant activities.

From the new charts, the team developed a flow map to capture the interrelationships of work within the department in a visual format. (See Figure 2 on pages 96 and 97.)

This analysis process was difficult, tedious, and took the team almost two full months to complete. This was partially due to difficulties the team was having with its group process: Scheduling meetings was difficult, so they were constantly being postponed; team members were frequently absent or not prepared; and the attitudes expressed in the meetings were often negative.

A possible reason for the apparent drag in group process was that the HR director—perceived as the major advocate for the project—had announced that he would be leaving the division. This made many team members feel that continuing the redesign project would be a waste of their time. However, because the HR director's actual departure was not for several months, team members kept their reservations to themselves. A member of the redesign team recalled his [or her] feelings at the time:

> I really felt that the whole project should be cancelled. I mean here we were, the director is leaving, and we were trying to redesign the whole department. And we had no reason to believe the new director would want to hear our ideas about the department.

Customer Feedback Meeting: A Turning Point

To ensure the team was getting an accurate picture of the HR function, the project leader interviewed HR customers to determine value-added and non-value-added services. A cross-section of *positive* and *negative* customers was selected by the team, and a list of interview questions was developed. The interview results were very negative. In general, customers did not feel that HR was helpful, value-added, or customer-focused.

When the project leader presented the interview data to the redesign team, its reaction was one of total denial and disbelief. Several team members implied that the project leader had intentionally biased the interview results to make the department look bad. One member was so upset that he [or she] left the meeting. This member said he [or she] would have nothing more to do with the team. The rest of the team members were shocked at this, but they also shared those sentiments. The customer data was the last straw for them. They already felt the project was meaningless ever since the HR director announced he would be leaving. As a result, they suggested the project be put on hold.

The project leader recalled this difficult period of the project:

> I really thought it was over. The OD manager told me that things were just at a low point and that we could get them going again, but I was not convinced. I felt that I had been personally attacked by the team when they doubted the integrity of the customer interviews. That hurt me and shook my self-confidence. Looking back at it now, I can see how this was a necessary phase that the team needed to go through. It wasn't easy to maintain that perspective at the time!

The HR director was surprised to hear about the problems. The OD manager suggested that the director call the team together to give them the following talk.

> I want to set the record straight on one point right from the beginning. This project is not some academic exercise. I am dead serious about getting this redesign completed. I am convinced that a lot of the things that we do around here could be done more effectively. You have the chance to step back from the daily grind and take a look at what things we *should* be doing. This project is damn important! I see this project as the way we can get things back on track.

> The fact that I am leaving soon makes this redesign all the more important. I want to do everything in my power to see that my successor receives this organization in the best possible condition. As of now, it looks like I am going to be leaving next quarter. So I want the redesign to be completed by that time. You have made some good progress, now do whatever you have to do to finish it.

The director's pep talk to the team was a real turning point. After this session, the team voluntarily agreed to start meeting on a daily basis. Two new members were added, and they breathed more positive life into the team. With a sudden burst of energy, the team developed a vision for what the department should look like in the future.

New Organizational Form Takes Shape

Rather than divide department work along functional lines, a new flowchart was made, highlighting three broad categories: HR Specialist,

Figure 2: Current HR Department Work Flows

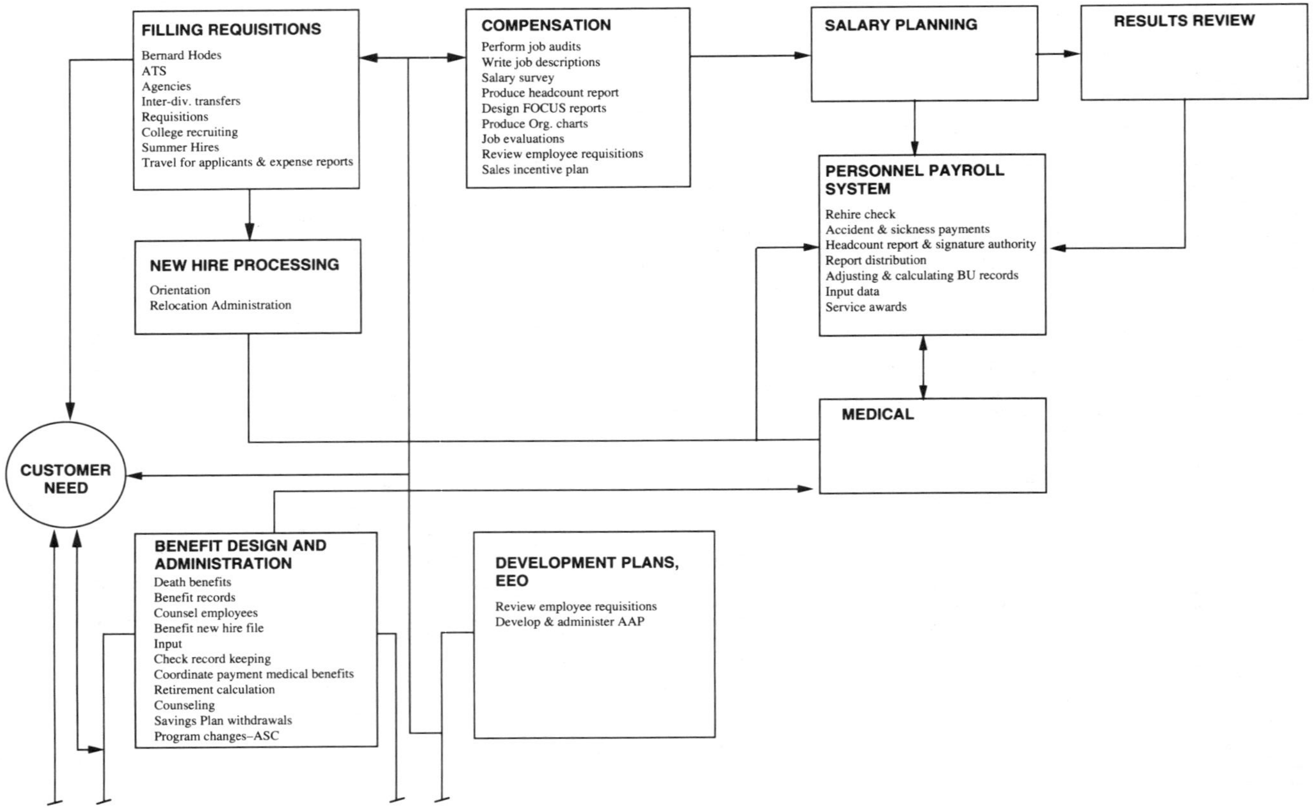

EMPLOYEE RELATIONS
Update salaried handbook
Administer discipline
General counseling
Leave abuse
General ER activities
Respond to complaints
Coordinate personnel policy revisions

EMPLOYEE SAFETY
Workers Comp

LABOR RELATIONS
Maintain BU job history
Administer & interpret labor agreement
Administer discipline
General counseling
Update BU handbook
BU job bids & promotion activity
BU auto-progression
Leave abuse
Review BU job descriptions
Quarterly BU attendance awards
BU labor reports
Labor negotiations

ATTITUDE SURVEY

PLANNING, RECRUITING FORECAST

TRAINING & DEVELOPMENT
Teach training
Coordination of training/administration
Education & teaching reimbursements
Management offsites
Design training programs
Matching funds

CAREER PLANNING

SUCCESSION PLANNING
MRP administration

HRC
HR plan
HR audit
Status and implement HR plan
Coordinate with HR functional areas

CAREER OPPORTUNITY PROGRAM

ADMINISTRATIVE/ GENERAL
Telephones   Emp. sales &
Filing   discount tickets
Mail/fax   Activity reports
Schedule meetings   Bereavement/
Type memos, etc.   jury duty
Travel arrangements
Expense reports
Maintain calendars
Order supplies

SPECIAL PROJECTS
Picnic   Xmas dinner
SAC   SOBC/COI cards
AQMD
All emp. mtgs.
Misc. task teams
Gainsharing
Ethics training
Drug program
Awards
Administer cafeteria services

EMPLOYEE COMMUNICATIONS
Suggestion program
UPDATE
Employee communication distribution

INTERNATIONAL SUPPORT
International compensation
Payroll and personnel records
Staffing
Foreign sales payments

EXIT
Exit interviews

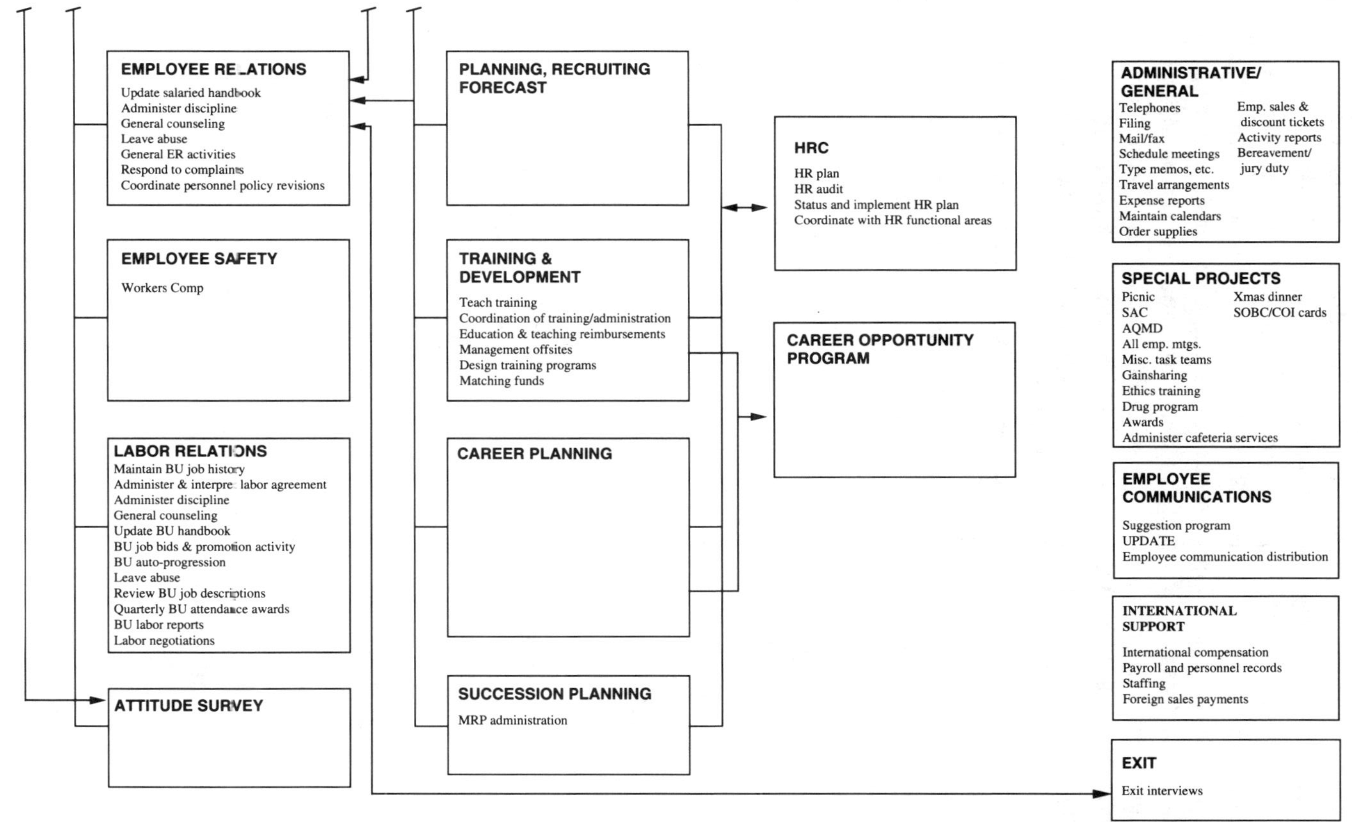

97

HR Consultant, and Administrative. These divisions constituted what the team saw as the three distinct types of departmental work.

When the work was reorganized into these three categories, the team developed some new insights. Many of the activities classified as specialist tasks required little more than specialist leadership. Some could be performed entirely by a high-level administrative person. This was an important insight because the specialists had been complaining about how much administrative work they were doing. Apparently, they were doing this work because they did not feel comfortable giving it to administrative people: They felt responsible for it.

Tasks were rearranged into the Redesign Configuration (RC) Chart shown as Figure 3 on pages 100 and 101.)

The RC chart became a vital working document. It was maintained on a large whiteboard, with each major work function represented by a 3M Post-it Note.™ Much of the redesign process involved revisions to this chart because it served as a representation of the whole HR work system.

One important feature of the RC chart was that it captured *work clusters;* that is, related work was grouped together in the boxes as indicated. Thus, each cluster provides a meaningful unit of work for the person(s) performing the tasks in a cluster. For example, in the Specialist box under the sub-heading Management, there are a number of work clusters: Review BU job descriptions, Update BU handbook, Leave abuse-BU, and Administer/interpret labor agreement comprise one work cluster. Job descriptions and job audits/job evaluations make up another cluster.

Once this macro-level depiction of the HR system was completed, the tasks within each of the sections were considered for redesign. If the team thought a task was inefficient, incompatible with the redesign team mission, or should be performed by another department, it was considered a possible opportunity for redesign.

A total of 44 redesign opportunities were identified. Of these, 39 tasks were identified for variance analysis. These were then classified into three categories based on the potential for improvement: 17 were considered High Priority; 14 were Medium Priority; and 8 were Low Priority. Using the variance analysis form shown as Figure 4 on the following page, team members interviewed employees who performed the work identified for variance analysis.

Variance sheets were presented by each team member to the redesign team. Recommendations for changes were discussed, and redesign improvements were quantified according to a best estimate. There were two general kinds of improvements: quantifiable improvements in specific work processes; and qualitative improvements in areas such as the department's image, improved teamwork, and ability to serve HR customers. Efficiency savings were estimated according to a simple formula:

Figure 4: Variance Analysis Chart

FUNCTION:

Variance	Causes	How is Variance Currently Controlled?	Recommended Changes	Benefit/Impact

an estimate of the savings per task multiplied by the frequency of the task to determine total savings.

Redesign Recommendations

The team's redesign recommendations were split into two categories: items for immediate action, which consisted of actions to address 12 of the Medium to High Priority opportunities; and second-tier opportunities. The first category of recommendations represented mostly efficiency savings. These savings resulted from the elimination of waste in predominantly linear processes. While it was more difficult to quantify savings from the second-tier recommendations, these comprised the most substantial part of the team's work. The total yearly estimated equivalent from the items for immediate action was one Full Time Equivalent (FTE—approximately 2,000 hours/year). Anticipated savings from the second-tier items was estimated at five FTEs (10,000 hours/year). In personnel costs alone, this translated into a savings of more than $300,000 per year.

In the second-tier recommendations, the team outlined the major elements of the redesign: a new organization structure, specific job descriptions for the Human Resource Consultants, plans for a departmental Central Services administrative function, an HR Helpline, and a new physical layout for the central HR department.

Organization Structure

The organizational structure recommended was a functional matrix. The HRCs in this structure have essentially two points of accountability: to the HR department and the director of their client functional area. And, because they have HR generalist responsibility, they can focus on providing proactive customer service rather than just performing specialist tasks.

Figure 3: HR Redesign—Macro Structure

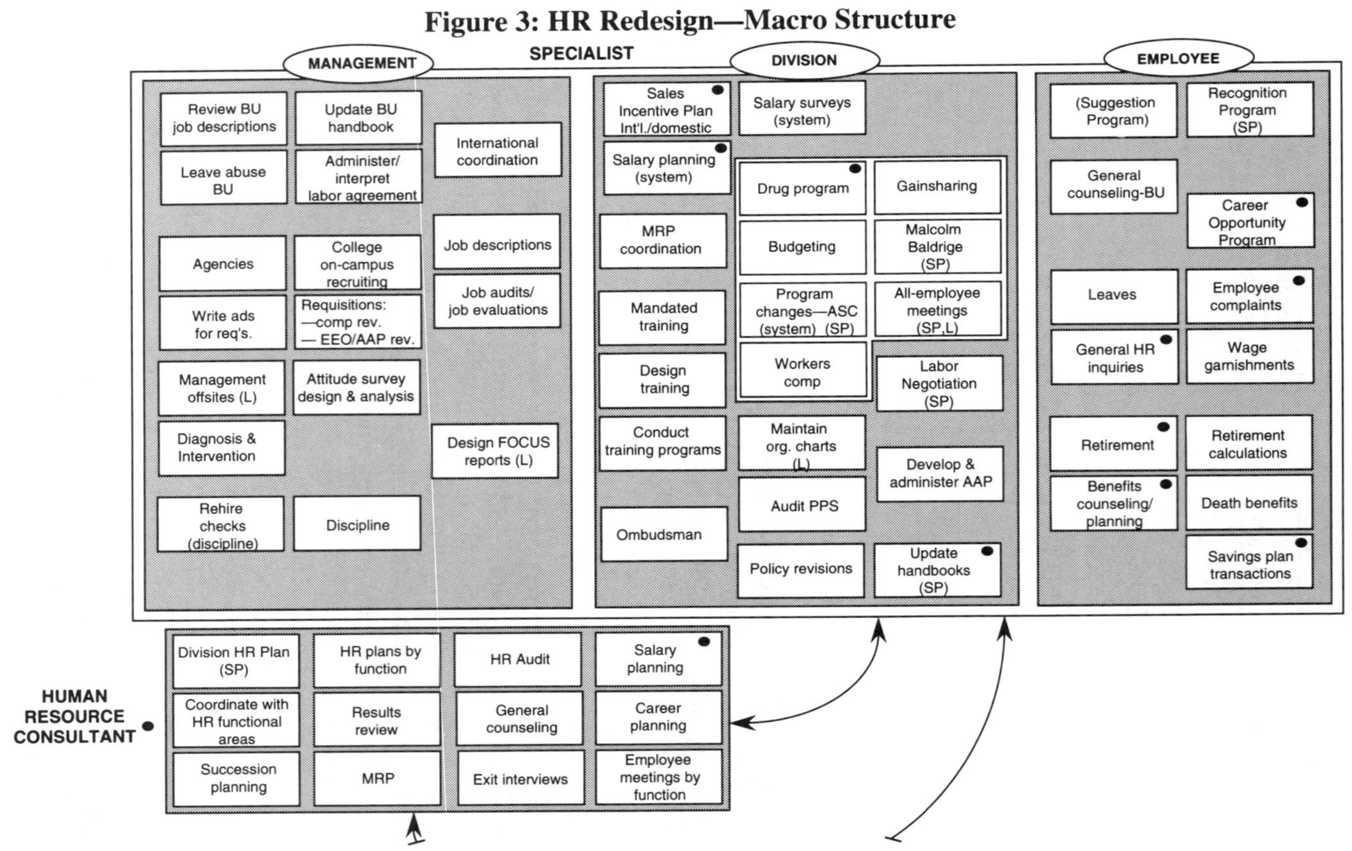

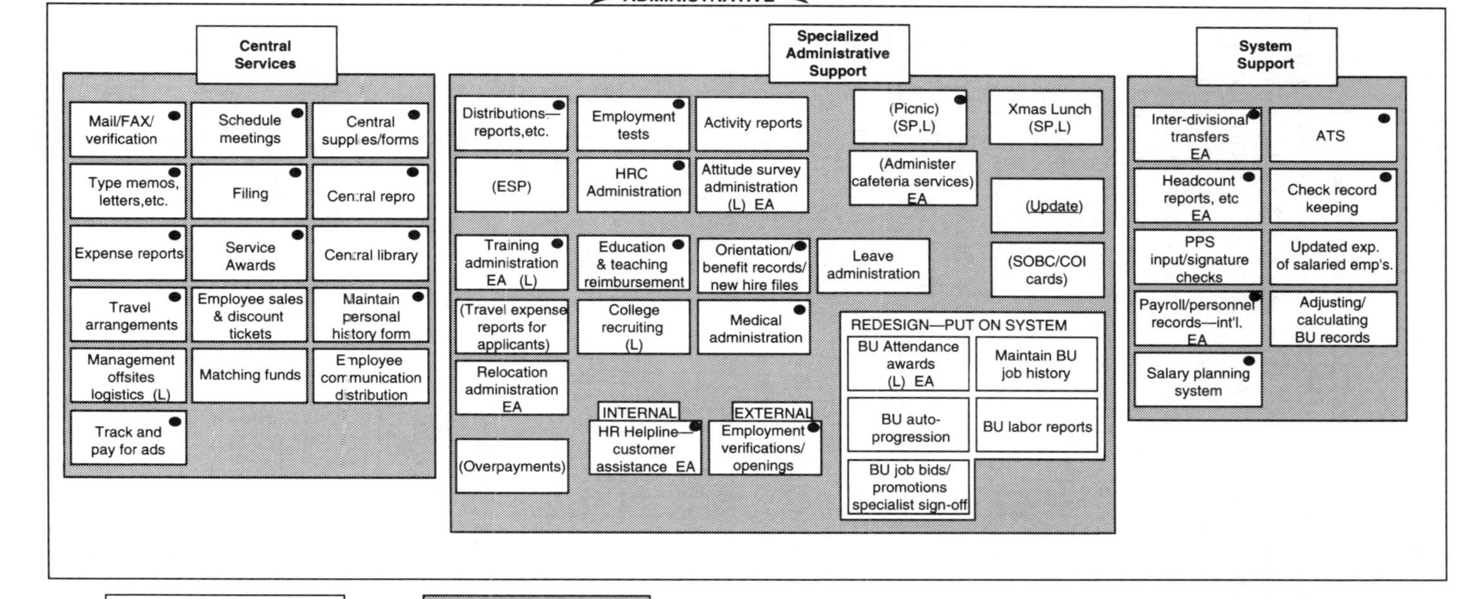

ADMINISTRATIVE

Central Services
Mail/FAX/ verification
Schedule meetings
Central supplies/forms
Type memos, letters,etc.
Filing
Central repro
Expense reports
Service Awards
Central library
Travel arrangements
Employee sales & discount tickets
Maintain personal history form
Management offsites logistics (L)
Matching funds
Employee communication distribution
Track and pay for ads

Specialized Administrative Support
Distributions—reports,etc.
Employment tests
Activity reports
(Picnic) (SP,L)
Xmas Lunch (SP,L)
(ESP)
HRC Administration
Attitude survey administration (L) EA
(Administer cafeteria services) EA
(Update)
Training administration EA (L)
Education & teaching reimbursement
Orientation/ benefit records/ new hire files
Leave administration
(SOBC/COI cards)
(Travel expense reports for applicants)
College recruiting (L)
Medical administration
REDESIGN—PUT ON SYSTEM
BU Attendance awards (L) EA
Maintain BU job history
Relocation administration EA
INTERNAL
HR Helpline— customer assistance EA
EXTERNAL
Employment verifications/ openings
BU auto-progression
BU labor reports
(Overpayments)
BU job bids/ promotions specialist sign-off

System Support
Inter-divisional transfers EA
ATS
Headcount reports, etc EA
Check record keeping
PPS input/signature checks
Updated exp. of salaried emp's.
Payroll/personnel records—int'l. EA
Adjusting/ calculating BU records
Salary planning system

KEY
SP = Special Project
L = Specialist Leadership Required
EA = Enriched Administrative
( ) = Move out of HR?
● = Redesign Opportunity?
⬯ = Source of Work

SPECIAL NOTES:
EQUIPMENT:
FAX MACHINE
VOICE MAIL
XEROX MACHINE
REVISIT OFFICE LAYOUT

The creation of the HRC position represented a significant growth opportunity for others in the HR organization.

HRC Role

The HRC job includes tasks traditionally performed by HR specialists, ranging from management development and EEO planning to staffing and recruitment forecasting. It was expected that the HRC would become a trusted confidant—looked to by the functional director for advice on significant, strategic HR issues. However, HRCs were cautioned not to become the source for *all* HR activity. Employees were still expected to work through the *main body* of the HR function for generic services such as benefits and retirement information. However, the HRC is the one-stop source for strategic HR issues.

Central Services

Due to the high degree of redundant administrative work being performed by specialists throughout HR, the design team recommended this work be centralized. Rather than maintain the traditional manager-secretary pairing that had existed in the department, the team called for the creation of a Central Services group, which would handle a large variety of administrative functions. In addition, this function would be responsible for the coordination of some enriched administrative tasks, which had previously been performed by specialists. One of these enriched positions was for a lead administrator to coordinate the Central Services function.

HR Helpline

The team suggested that a "hotline" number be set up to handle HR questions. The line could be expected to reduce the number of work interruptions due to employees calling the wrong individual within HR. In addition, the dedicated line would be a contact point for customers that would be manned at all times on a rotational basis. This would improve the department's image with customers who were frustrated by not being able to reach *the right person* in HR.

Physical Layout

The team considered the department's physical layout a major source of internal conflict. They also felt the sprawling and fragmented layout presented an unprofessional image to customers. The current layout was contributing to the high level of work interruptions, low levels of confidentiality, and poor teamwork. Employees in each separate hallway had their own coffee machines and tended to develop into cliquey groups. There was a clear rift between those in Staffing, Benefits, and Employee Relations. Much of this was attributed to the fact that these groups rarely interacted informally with each other.

The changes suggested in the physical layout were to bring the entire department into one area and control departmental access—thus, physically controlling the flow of work into the department. The professional offices formed the perimeter around the Central Services function.

Discussion

Project Leader's Parting Thoughts

The project leader had seen the team go through many changes during the redesign process. The project had gotten off to a rocky start, but he felt pleased with the results.

> This process has taught me a lot about working in groups and the technical process of doing work redesign. In the administrative environment, there is no clear road map to guide you through the process. In school they tell you that you need to "trust in the process." The problem is that when that advice is most true is when it's the most difficult to believe—how can you trust a process when you aren't sure that it's taking you where you want to go?

> The new HR director hasn't been around to see the pain that this team went through in coming up with its recommendations. He seemed receptive to the team's presentation the other day. I am just afraid that he will not be able to fully implement the team's recommendations. If that happens, it will be a long time before anybody around here gets involved in another task team.

Case Reflections

Some of the first-tier efficiency opportunities have been successfully implemented. The more substantial second-tier effectiveness opportunities are just beginning to be implemented. If the second-tier opportunities—new organization structure, HRC roles, Central Services, the HR helpline, and the physical layout changes—are not eventually addressed, the project will fail to bring about the transformative changes sought through the redesign process. Instead, it will have resulted in relatively minor efficiency gains which do nothing to make the organization fundamentally more effective. In fact, the efficiency savings that were gained through the first-tier opportunities represent real savings only if the time saved is used productively.

The only way that real savings can result is for the department to undergo the second-tier transformative changes. As the department is transformed, the members develop new attitudes about their work (i.e., the social system is changed). Opportunities for continual learning on the job and application of one's unique skills encourage individuals to contribute higher levels of energy and commitment to the organization. Operational savings gained from task efficiencies can help employees to achieve yet higher levels of performance and strategically benefit the business. When this occurs, the organization will have been transformed into a self-renewing high performance system.

To live up to the initial expectations for the project, the recommendations need to be implemented as a total system. The more the recommendations are tweaked and twisted, the greater the risk that they will not embody the fundamental systems change suggested by the redesign team. For example, *cherry-picking* recommendations such as centralizing administrative services without changing the physical layout will not provide the same impact as if the changes were made in tandem. The redesign team took an open systems perspective in their recommendations; thus, the interconnectedness of the changes cannot be overlooked during implementation.

Conclusion

This chapter has attempted to integrate theoretical and practical perspectives on work redesign to suggest some basic advice to those redesigning staff functions. The redesign process discussed is conceptually straightforward—ten basic steps—but the application of this change process becomes much more complex, as is illustrated in this case study.

OD practitioners working in systems redesign need to take more time to document and publish their successes and failures. This is particularly true in the nonlinear white-collar arena. It is only through presentation of cases such as this that redesign models for staff functions (e.g., Mumford, 1983; Pava, 1983) can be tested and refined. It is hoped that others will be stimulated to pursue this objective.

References

Cummings, T.G. "Socio-technical Systems: An Intervention Strategy." In *Socio-technical Systems: A Sourcebook,* edited by W.A. Pasmore & J.J. Sherwood. La Jolla: University Associates, 1976.

Emery, F.E., & Trist, E.L. "Socio-technical systems." In *Management Science: Models and Techniques,* edited by C.W. Churchman & Verhulst. New York: Pergamon, 1960.

Hanna, D.P. *Designing Organizations for High Performance.* Reading: Addison-Wesley, 1988.

Mumford, E. *Designing Human Systems for New Technology: The ETHICS Method.* Manchester: Manchester Business School, 1983.

Pasmore, W.A. *Designing Effective Organizations: The Socio-technical Systems Perspective.* New York: John Wiley, 1988.

Pava, C.H.P. *Managing New Office Technology: An Organizational Strategy.* New York: Free Press, 1983.

Sherwood, J.J. "Creating Work Cultures with Competitive Advantage." *Organizational Dynamics,* (1988): pp. 5-26.

Additional Related Materials

Pava, C.H.P. "Redesigning Socio-technical Systems Design: Concepts and Methods for the 1990s." *The Journal of Applied Behavioral Science,* 22 no. 3, (1986): pp. 201-221.

Perrow, C. "The Bureaucratic Paradox: The Efficient Organization Centralizes in Order to Decentralize." *Organizational Dynamics,* (Spring, 1977): pp. 3-14.

Susman, G.I and Chase, R.B. "A Socio-technical Analysis of the Integrated Factory." *The Journal of Applied Behavioral Science,* 22 no. 3, (1986): pp. 257-270.

Taylor, J.C. "Long-term Socio-technical Systems Change in a Computer Operations Department." *The Journal of Applied Behavioral Science,* 22 no. 3, (1986): pp. 303-313.

Van Wagenen Keil, S. "Designing America's New Corporate Culture." *The Tarrytown Letter,* no. 48, (April, 1985): p. 18.

Weisbord, M.R. *Productive Workplaces: Organizing and Managing for Dignity, Meaning, and Community.* San Francisco: Jossey-Bass, 1989.

8. Ethnographic Work Modeling Interventions

Larrie D. Loehr

An Intervention

"Our company should aim for no injuries, no accidents! We want an accident-free workplace! We may not achieve zero accidents, but we are more likely to reduce them if our goal is zero," said Kathy, the regional president.

I could scarcely believe it. We normally have 20-25 accidents yearly. To have no accidents would be a radical change. And I'm somewhat skeptical of statements about needs for radical change. So I checked with the corporate executive vice president. "Is Kathy really committed to this? Is the corporation really serious?"

"Absolutely. We want to rapidly transform the safety behavior of all 12,000 employees!"

So I decided this would be an interesting and worthwhile change. It would be a system-wide change; a strategic change with full corporate support. I said, "Kathy, I know ways for rapidly transforming the behavior of the 2,000 employees in our two-state region. Are you serious? Do you want me to start?"

"Do it!" she said.

So I did. That's an intervention—the "do it" part.

The intervention was to quickly and significantly reduce accidents in our 2,000-member subsidiary company. This was a tough challenge, since we were already a high performer and safer than the industry average.

Top management contracted for the intervention. They did not specify how to do it, so it was up to me to use the methods I thought were best for accomplishing the desired result. This would be a test of making an actual *intervention* in the workplace. It would be the next step in the organization development process after entry, analysis, and contracting. My actions were expected to directly and rapidly lead to reducing accidents.

I was sure I could achieve this because of my confidence in making the intervention. I had strong organization development skills and had been developing a new, powerful kind of intervention: ethnographic work modeling.

Less than one year later, accidents in our 2,000-person workforce decreased 28 percent. Our company also improved its standing relative to

---

Larrie Loehr is Assistant Manager of Training & Safety, Central Telephone Company of Virginia and North Carolina, P.O. Box 6788, Charlottesville, VA 22906.

other companies, reversing a three-year downward trend. Thus, we improved both *absolutely* and *comparatively.*

Behind the statistics, decreased accidents meant one employee probably was saved from a permanently disabling injury or death, and nine others from serious injury. The quality of communication improved too. All four of the company's regional union presidents compared this improvement to tearing down the Berlin Wall. They had never met with management to participate in developing an overall strategy for improvement! Improved communications came from working together on safety.

My intent here is to briefly portray the impetus and results of one intervention. The next section describes the structure and rationale for the ethnographic work modeling intervention I used. This is followed by a detailed description of four applications of this type of intervention and a list of other application areas. The last section provides a critique of ethnographic interventions and directions for the future.

Ethnographic Work Modeling Interventions
Concepts and Techniques

> "You missed a great public-channel TV show last night. Two guys were talking about how to improve quality and productivity. They really understood how to do it. First time I heard anyone talk sensibly about it. Sounds like they do what you try to do. You ought to look them up!"

When my father-in-law says that, I listen. He is a pessimist. A retired surgeon and psychiatrist, he is not positive about survival prospects for the human race or improvements in the quality and productivity of U.S. companies' products and services. He continued.

> "These two guys talked about what accounts for good work— respect for the individual, the desire to do quality work, the destructive effect of how business organizations treat individuals, and the effect this treatment has on products and services. They also have solutions. That's what made their TV appearance remarkable. They're on the right track."

I was determined to find out what was so wonderful. And there it was, 30 minutes away at the University of Virginia. An acquaintance of mine, a professor at the McIntire School of Commerce, Gib Akin, had been conducting original research into cultural approaches to productivity. Drawing on psychology and anthropology, he and a colleague, David Hopelain, had formulated an ethnographic approach to work for improving productivity (Akin & Hopelain, 1986; Akin, 1987). The Public Broadcasting Corporation heard about this approach and featured them on a TV panel discussion.

I called Gib and for the next three years he and Dave shared their research with me. We did various projects. We also started a nonprofit educational and research corporation called The Center For Study of the Meaning of Work, an organizational umbrella for some of our efforts. I absorbed the ethnographic framework of thinking into my own activities and began ethnographic interventions where I worked. Meanwhile, Gib added areas of application to strategic planning, supervisory training, and recognition programs (Akin & Lee, 1990; Akin & Schultheiss, 1990).

I now think of ethnographic work modeling interventions as based on concepts and techniques that can be used in a variety of ways for improving work. These interventions are a way of looking at organizational life—a perspective or lens—that affects both perception and thinking.

I see and think of an organization as a group of people possessing knowledge about how to get work done. As an anthropologist looks at a tribe, I look at an organization as a tribe and a work group as a clan within the tribe. Tribes and clans have their own culture—a shared body of knowledge they use to make sense of their life and as a basis of acting. Ethnography provides a way to learn that culture.

Ethnography literally means the *study of culture.* A detailed description of ethnographic techniques is in James Spradley's *The Ethnographic Interview* (1979). The perspective is to understand a culture from the native point of view,

> to grasp the native's point of view, his relation to life, to realize *his* vision of *his* world.... Rather than *studying people,* ethnography means *learning from people* (p. 3).

Anyone who aspires to use ethnographic interventions should read Spradley's book. It provides specific guidelines and examples of data collection and analysis.

The next section describes the concepts and techniques of the ethnographic work model, and explains how to use them in a variety of applications and results. For easy reading, I will use the term *ethnographic interventions* interchangeably with *ethnographic work modeling interventions.*

The Concepts

Concepts of ethnographic work modeling interventions deal with definitions of the culture of the workplace. The ethnographic approach is defined as a perspective or lens for understanding an organization as a culture. *Culture* is defined as the shared collection of knowledge that organizational members use to understand the workplace and guide their actions. *Productivity* and *quality* are defined as the ability to get work done well. Finally, there is a specific body of knowledge about productivity and quality in each organization, defined as the *culture of productivity* (Akin & Hopelain, 1986). This culture can be accessed through ethnographic techniques.

The Techniques

Techniques of ethnographic interventions consist of principles of interventions, work modeling, measurement, and implementation planning.

■ Principles of interventions.

— Focus attention on work. Look at knowledge pertaining to work itself—not structure—interpersonal issues, goals, etc. Narrowly focus on work (e.g., the work of safety, the work of understanding a specification manual, the work of inputting data).

— Build on strengths—what is going right. Look at good work; that way you will find the knowledge that accounts for success, not failure. Managers may object to this on the grounds that one has to find the problem (i.e., what's wrong) first. Focusing on problems and what's wrong wastes time and is de-energizing. This is a trap, because then you will spend time finding the culture of failure, instead of solutions. Solutions are already there, if you focus on them! So, recognize good work rather than failure. And recognize the knowledge that makes success happen.

— Introduce change as experiments. Load your intervention for success by launching it as an experiment. Aim to both improve results and learn new information about what to do in the future.

— Emphasize participation. Include members of the organization or work group in planning and doing the intervention. Participation is necessary because improvements are done by work group members, and only they have the required knowledge. Without their participation, there is nobody who can do the improvement.

— Adopt philosophy of small wins. Going for small rather than big improvements minimizes resistance, attracts resources, gets results faster, is less risky, and easier to manage.

■ Work modeling—how good work gets done.

— Emphasizes descriptions, not judgments; strengths, not problems; meaning, not explanation; what and how, not why.

— Use graphics. Construct a picture or drawing of the specific work culture. Consider a collage or multi-colored lists of items with arrows showing how elements of the culture relate. Use artistic imagination. The objective is to present a depiction or model of the specific work culture, so members of the culture can see it, amend and verify it, and use it as a reference point in later discussions.

■ Measurement of results. In focusing on strengths, you can always identify indicators people use to tell how work is going. Those are measurements. Those are the everyday measurements people use to know the quality of their work. These indicators help them do their jobs and are used to communicate to outsiders how they are doing, and they use the workers' local knowledge. Finally, different work groups will use different measures to know how other work groups are doing. So, there will be multiple measurements for the multiple constituencies within the organization. Different measurements help different people get their work done.

■ Implementation Planning. Force-field analysis is a useful way to structure discussion about how to introduce the intervention. The ideal is to identify forces helping and restraining implementation of the experiment and to decrease restraining forces. Identify who will be hurt and who will be helped by the intervention, as well as steps you can take in advance to reduce the hurts. (Making it an experiment helps lessen fear of being hurt.)

Ethnographic Work Modeling Applications

This section describes four applications and lists potential in several other areas. Most applications are tactical; that is, they are used with a specific work group and not organization-wide. This is consistent with the techniques, which call for making small changes, maximizing learning from such changes, and avoiding "transformational" or major change as too risky and complex. The tactical applications include restructuring the organization of work in a work group from being supervisor-led to self-managed; improving the performance of a work group; and improving the quality of technical training.

The first application, however, describes a strategic application — one with an organization-wide focus and an intentional major change effort (described by top management as a *rapid transformational change*). This application was backed by a full array of organizational resources. The focus is on the work of safety.

Strategic: Initiating Transformational Organizational Change

Kathy said, "Do it! Rapidly transform the safety behavior of our 2,000 employees!"

I responded, "I'll start."

During our intervention discussion on measurements, we agreed that a 15 percent reduction in accidents within six months would show how much safety work improved and would, therefore, be a satisfactory indicator of rapidly changed behavior. The actual reduction was 28 percent. This was a strong indicator of a successful, system-wide, strategic transformation in safety behavior.

So what did I *do?* What was the intervention? More specifically, what did I do when I combined ethnographic concepts and techniques with my organization development skills to structure the intervention for a strategic, rapid transformation?

I started the intervention by calling a conference of key stakeholders — all top management, the safety group, and chairs of existing safety committees. The purpose was to decide (in one day) on the goals, structure, and training necessary to improve safety. (This plan was adapted and modified from Kilmann, 1989.)

The conference design was an application of the concepts and principles of interventions, work modeling, measurement, and implementation planning to the work of safety. The design focused on strengths, rather than problems.

The conference started with presentations and clarifying discussions of The Virginia Safety Organization and The North Carolina Safety Organization. Figure 1 shows the conference agenda distributed in advance to participants.

Figure 1: NC/VA Safety Summit Conference

NC/VA Safety Summit Conference

"Safety in 1990"

Achieving Safety Excellence

Through

Training, Structure, & Goals

October 24, 1989

The Dutch Inn, Martinsville, Virginia

AGENDA

10:00 Introduction—J. Thomas Brown
Presentations & Clarifying Discussions:
The Virginia Safety Organization
—VA Safety Coordinator with Virginia Group
The North Carolina Safety Organization
—NC Safety Coordinator with North Carolina Group

11:30 **Safety Concerns/Issues—Panel Discussion**
NC/VA Safety Specialists with NC/VA Participants

12:00 **Improvement Suggestions I—Henry Harper**
Presentations, Group Discussion & Recommendations
Training for 1990 Safety
—Short Presentation by Safety Specialists
—NC, VA, Staff—Review & Report

1:30 Light Buffet Lunch and/or Exercise

2.30 **Improvement Suggestions II—Larry Houck**
Presentations, Group Discussion & Recommendations
Structure & Goals for 1990 Safety
—Short Presentation by Safety Specialists
—NC, VA, Staff—Review, Report & Approve

5:30 **Comments About Conference**
All Groups, Tom Brown Summary and Farewell

6:00 Depart

The presentations were based on the "Models of Safety Success" for each state (see Figures 2 and 3 on pages 112 and 113). These models were derived from ethnographic interviews and observations prior to

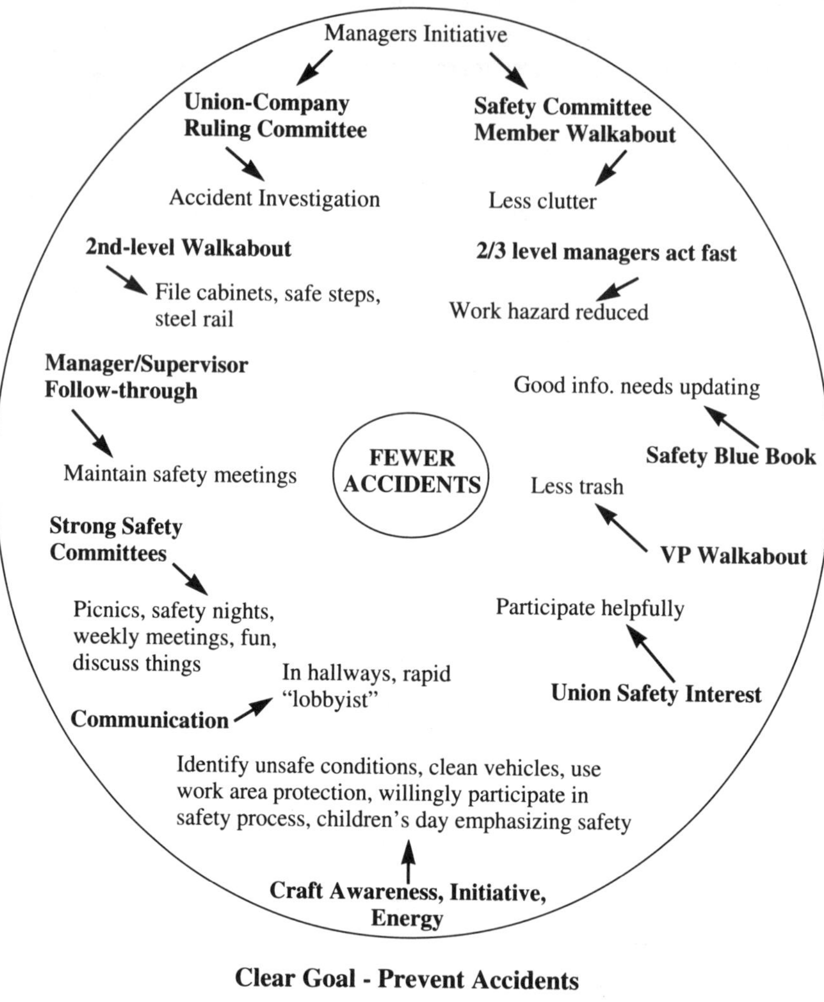

the conference. They were the models of the culture of safety success in each state.

The discussion of the strengths of the safety culture energized the stakeholder groups. They refined the models (verification) and identified the problems that blocked the successes of the culture. Then they generated suggestions for strengthening the existing culture of success by adapting changes in goals, structure, and training. Finally, a schedule for implementation was decided.

The results were indicated by multiple measures ranging from participant reactions and learning to behavioral and structural changes that indicated successful overall reductions in organization accidents. These results were achieved through a combination of ethnographic and organi-

Figure 3: North Carolina Model of Safety Success

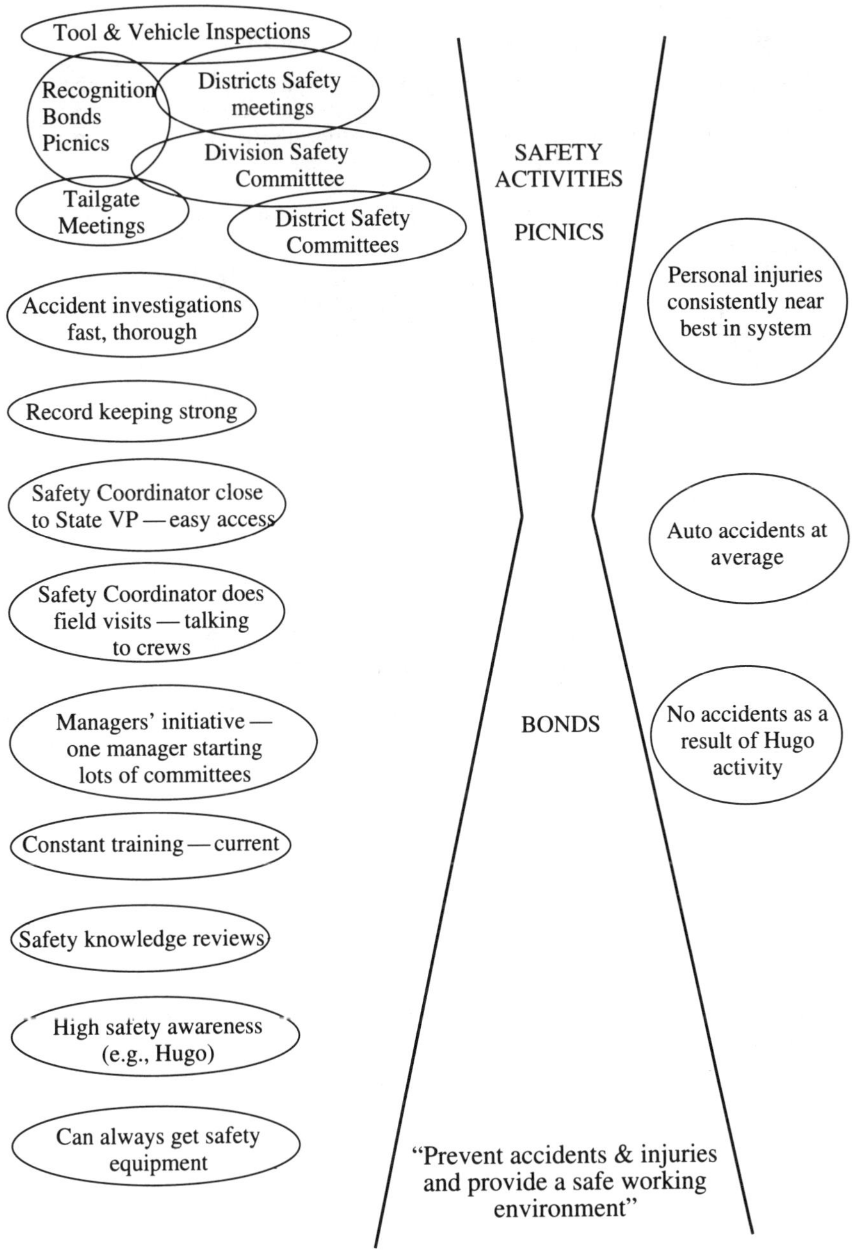

zation development methods. The point, however, is to illustrate the successful use of a specific ethnographic intervention; that is, one grounded in the culture of success that was uncovered in the *ethnographic* field work.

Tactical: Restructuring the Organization of Work

Poor performance of the word-processing unit became an unscheduled topic at the company's annual planning conference. The complaints were low quality work, unmet deadlines, and discourteous customer treatment. The unhappy customers were the managers. My job was to improve the situation.

Results: The next year the unit and I were commended at the conference. The managers noted a remarkable turnaround. Work was virtually without errors, on time, and customers were treated politely. The managers didn't know how it happened; only that the results were outstanding. I didn't present back-up data, although it was there:

■ Productivity. Lines per hour increased 62 percent, and the supervisor was released for other duties.

■ Quality. Error-free rates rose to 99.53 percent; on-time rates rose to 99.4 percent; and new surveys showed improved customer satisfaction.

■ Growth. New business was generated. Total lines increased 37 percent and special projects increased 312 percent, yet overtime went up only three hours. Compared to the prior three years, the unit produced 16 percent more lines with 28 percent fewer employees! Afterwards, the unit managed itself through monthly reports and a bi-monthly meeting with a manager.

Using ethnographic work modeling, I was able to restructure the group as a self-managed unit after two, two-hour meetings. There were three parts to the intervention: design and implementation of the meeting agenda, scheduling of the actions to take, and overall implementation guidelines. The work unit measured the results.

My first step was to learn the work of the group and identify its strengths. The next steps were to develop a graphic work model, verify it with the group, and ask for ways to improve the work using the strengths. During steps one and two, I gathered the people in the group, suggested work could be done better if they were more self-managing, and set an agenda for the meeting to design a structure for self-management. The agenda was designed to help define self-management; identify unit strengths; identify obstacles to success; identify actions to remove, overcome, or sidestep obstacles; describe success and how to measure it; and describe necessary actions. I then provided implementation guidelines.

■ Focus on work.

■ Do improvements as small experiments, not policy changes.

■ Describe the specifics of success and its measurement—don't look for problems or ask why.

■ Learn from what happens when you act and measure.

■ Decide whether to expand after acting.

They agreed, followed the agenda, and started. Obstacles occurred as anticipated. For example, a union official nearly filed a labor grievance. Some managers said they didn't like the idea of a self-managed work group. But the unit drew on its strengths. Members reminded the critics this was only an experiment, the results were good, and we should go one more month.

At the end of the second month, customers reported dramatically improved results, so we decided to continue the self-managed work group indefinitely with monthly review meetings. Adverse comments by union and management diminished. Our success was recognized eight months later, when managers attending a company conference noted the improved service (Loehr, 1988).

Tactical: Performance Improvement

"We can't seem to get address data coded accurately into the new data base," said the manager of one of the coding units. "And that means we won't be able to automatically assign customers' telephone lines to the right telephone cable. There will be too many errors."

The new system affected 350,000 customers' addresses. I suggested we conduct an experiment to improve accuracy. The managers reluctantly agreed. When I mentioned we would do an ethnographic productivity improvement project, I lost credibility and nearly lost the opportunity to conduct the project. (One lesson: Don't use the word ethnographic!) However the managers said,

"The bottom line is to reduce the 4-to-9 percent daily error rates. Our current errors will make the data bank useless. GIGO is taking over. Garbage in is garbage out! We've got to do something!"

So I proceeded with the ethnographic intervention. Four weeks later, error rates dropped to 1.8 percent or lower and stayed there.

The intervention quickly used all the techniques — principles of interventions, work modeling, measurement, and implementation planning. The principles were used particularly well. There was focused attention on work; the experiment built on strengths — what was going right; change was introduced as an experiment; the whole work group participated; and the philosophy of small wins was used, though perhaps not enough.

What happened? The two consultants described the experiment to the six-member work group, then observed and interviewed the members for about two days. The observation and interviews followed the ethnographic procedures described by Spradley (1979). This data was then turned into a picture, or model, of the culture of inputting accurate data. After all, they were doing it right 90 percent of the time already!

Two meetings were then held with the work group. The first meeting presented the model, and the group verified it. Small changes were made. The members developed a shared understanding of what they did when they performed successful work.

The second meeting identified ways to improve the accuracy of coding. These improvements were based on the members' strengths as identified in the model. Internal and external measurements were identified, including using the daily error rate and implementation scheduled over the next two weeks.

The key suggestions for improvement were small changes the members could make in the way they shared information about proper coding. They proposed much quicker and informal methods such as posting a flip chart in the workroom so they could write down new codes for everyone to see, instead of holding them privately.

The work group also experienced a burst of energy with one member saying, "Management doesn't let us do good work. Do you know how awful it is to wake up in the morning and go to work knowing you can't do good work because management will not let you? All they want is speed. But you know much of your work will have to be redone because the data is inaccurate."

The members now saw a way they could change their situation, and they did. The results were dramatic. Accuracy and productivity improved with more information being loaded into the data bank with greater accuracy. Daily error rates went from 4-9 percent to under 1.8 percent, for an average 361 percent improvement. For several months I kept in contact with the group and found the reduced rates sustained.

Positive side effects were noted too. There was more consistent address input from other offices because members started to export their new informal methods of sharing information to other work groups.

One result was that the group never received formal recognition. Then it was disbanded at the conclusion of the project. The participants, however, continued to remember their accomplishments. One person said he looked back at that time as one of excitement and being deeply satisfied because he was allowed to do good work. Another result led to the next improvement project.

Tactical: Training Improvement

This intervention is not as clear as others. Its value is that it illustrates a unique application of an ethnographic intervention.

Recall that the knowledge of what accounts for success can be known and accessed through the concepts and techniques of ethnographic interventions. From this, it can be reasoned that the knowledge of what was done to learn that knowledge can also be known. There is a culture of learning itself. *This learning culture can be accessed by observation and interviews focusing on what was done to learn how to accomplish good work* (Akin, 1987).

The product from this type of ethnographic intervention is a model of learning for the particular work culture. In this instance, after the knowledge of accurate data coding was obtained and verified, a second round of interviews and observations was conducted. The purpose was to identify what the members of the group did to learn how to successfully code data.

One product from this learning was a verified "Craftpersons Lucas Learning Model." (See Figure 4.)

Figure 4: Craftpersons Lucas Learning Model

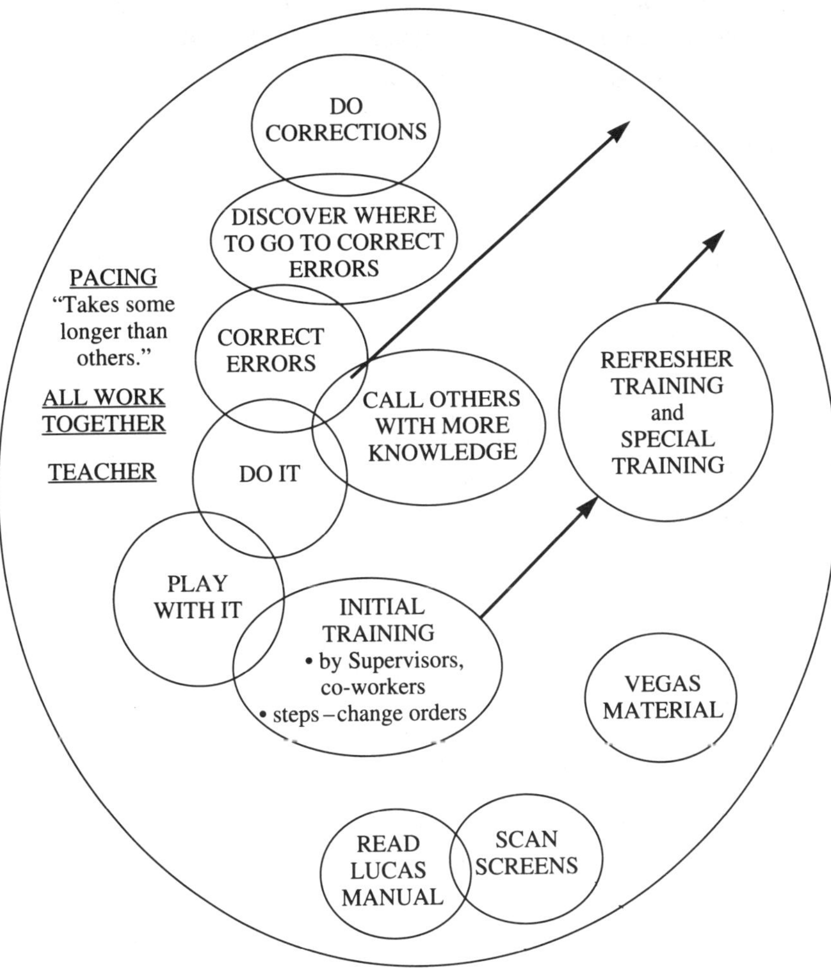

A second product was a list of the technical skill competencies for performing the work. Third was a written guide for newcomers and staff for on-the-job and refresher training. In addition, a report called *Technical Skills Training For LUCAS Users* was written for management and presented to the Operations president.

The products were used by other work groups and received favorable ratings in terms of reactions and learning outcomes. Performance improved in terms of higher quality work, indicated by improved "flow through rates," a measure of the degree to which data was processed by the system automatically without manual assistance. Another organizational impact was that the training products were distributed to work groups in other business units, and a decision was made at corporate levels to develop a formal training program based on ethnographic techniques.

Current and Prospective Application Areas

Ethnographic interventions have been completed or are underway in the following application areas.

- Strategic
— Strategic planning
— Community relations
— Safety
- Tactical
— Building design
— Contractor specification manuals
— Customer service productivity
— Performance recognition
— Procurement specifications for local area computer networks (LANs)
— Recruitment
— Sales
— Supervisor training

Documentation of results is scarce. Almost all information in the public domain is listed in the references. Much of the work is located in private or proprietary publications such as the application of ethnographic interventions to improve the procurement of personal computers for an office of public affairs in a major organization. One potential bidder praised the final criteria for selection because it was so clear the company decided not to bid and saved resources for all concerned.

Critique: Issues, Prospective Applications, the Future

The concepts and techniques of ethnographic interventions combine to form a method for making organizational improvements. Their key advantages are that they can be used for any kind of improvement; they usually arouse little opposition and much enthusiasm among the participants; they are measurable and usually successful—sometimes extraordinarily successful.

So, why aren't these interventions used more? There are two issues: One is conceptual, and the other is the high level of skill required.

Conceptual Issue

First, it is difficult to use the in-place culture as the only source for improvement. This closed-system thinking could be remedied by identifying another organization's culture of success generating and using innovative ideas. Those strengths could then be used as interventions to improve the improvement process. This was done with powerful effect in the safety intervention, when members of one organization visited the work site of another organization for presentations, direct observation, and interviews. The CEO of the host organization led the presentation, demonstrating the culture of top management involvement with the improvement process.

A second difficulty concerns recognition. The indicators of success used by members of work groups are often different than those who control the resources of the group. Resources, therefore, may not be allocated to continue or strengthen the intervention even though local measurements indicate adequate or superior payback. Higher management, for its own reasons, may de-prioritize local organizational improvements and reduce resources for local interventions.

More strategic examples of ethnographic interventions would be useful. I am only aware of the limited example here in safety and another by my colleague Gib Akin, where a manufacturer is using the process to revise the mission of the company and its strategic marketing plan.

I have learned, however, to distrust strategic system-wide improvement approaches. I have seen and studied such efforts, designed and helped lead some of them, and been among those at whom changes are aimed. I think there is insufficient knowledge to conduct intentional system-wide change that will produce results anywhere near the intended outcomes. Organizational life is too complicated. The long time spans for strategic change provide opportunities for other variables to influence outcomes that cloud cause-and-effect relationships.

There is not enough knowledge to understand and direct strategic system-wide change in a comprehensive, competent manner. (Reference: Numerous private discussions among the author, Gib Akin, and Dave Hopelain from 1986-1990.) Theoretically, however, strategic system-wide knowledge is there, waiting to be discovered.

High-Level Skill Requirements

It appears self-serving to say ethnographic interventions require a high level of skill. Does that mean only specially-trained initiates can do it? Not quite.

Akin and Lee (1990) trained six supervisors in four workshops lasting a half-day each, plus a two-hour individual consultation. They found supervisors looked at their world differently and acted in ways more likely to enhance quality and productivity. Organizational results showed quality and productivity improvements, reductions in call backlogs, and reduced field rework. They concluded that, "Ethnographic methods used in more formal research can be used by supervisors to investigate their own settings."

The supervisors and their manager continue doing ethnographic interventions. Thus, elementary skills of ethnographic interventions can be taught to supervisors, and they can use these to make improvements in their work.

The ability to make ethnographic interventions in application areas other than intact work groups is more difficult to learn. My hunch is that skills for specific applications of ethnographic interventions can be learned relatively easily. However, learning to use those interventions in a broad range of applications is probably a professional-level skill.

Basic knowledge can be learned from the references in this chapter. Skill development would rest partly on an individual's prior experience in typical organization development activities (e.g., force-field analysis or team training). Skill development can occur through coaching from those doing ethnographic interventions.

For example, a student working on her MBA did a six-month, part-time internship with me as part of her MBA program. I felt she understood ethnographic interventions, could use that knowledge in various applications, and could also teach it. My student also was qualified professionally. She had a master's degree in education, ten years experience as a teacher, and additional years as a school administrator and manager in the private sector. Thus, interest and accomplishments in research are, for me, a requirement to practicing wide-ranging ethnographic interventions.

These issues of ethnographic interventions can be overcome. Energy for remedying the conceptual difficulties may come from either researchers or private sector organizations that see such interventions as a way to enhance quality and productivity better than current approaches.

The skill deficiencies can be remedied by training. Resources for training will be forthcoming if, or when, the results from ethnographic interventions are better documented and accepted.

Meanwhile, there are many application areas being explored now, and more are coming. I think there are promising applications for ethnographic work modeling interventions in the following areas:

- Design of operations and policy manuals.

- Interior design of work spaces.

- Mergers and acquisitions.

The Future

I find myself repeatedly asking, "Ethnographic interventions: What are they, and are they worthwhile?"

> "Larrie, what about those guys I mentioned several years ago. Did they have the answer to this country's problems about doing good work?"

My father-in-law never gives up on this subject. The country is always getting worse. I ask myself, "Will ethnographic interventions save it?"

I think we are on the right track. After four years, I see these interventions complement, not supplement, the country's emphasis on quality work. I believe the ethnographic way of looking at organizations will increasingly grip people's understanding of what's happening, and what they can do. While my own efforts have not produced wide-ranging improvements in organizational products or services, I have experienced some wonderful epiphanies. I am also encouraged by the progress of Gib Akin's reports. (See his current article, "Jazz Bands and Missionaries: OD Through Stories and Metaphors.")

References

Akin, Gib. "Varieties of Managerial Learning." *Organizational Dynamics,* (Autumn 1987).

Akin, Gib and Hopelain, David. "Finding The Culture of Productivity." *Organizational Dynamics,* (Winter 1986).

Akin, Gib and Lee, David. "Supervisory Training in a New Key." *Business,* (January-March 1990).

Akin, Gib and Schultheiss, Emily. "Jazz Bands and Missionaries: OD Through Stories and Metaphors." *Journal of Managerial Psychology,* 5 no. 4, (1990).

Kilmann, Ralph. "A Completely Integrated Program for Creating and Maintaining Organizational Success." *Organizational Dynamics,* (Summer 1989).

Loehr, Larrie. "Improving Work: Ethnographic Work Modeling and Results: A Description of Ethnographic Work Modeling and a 62 Percent Improvement from an Application in a Word-Processing Unit." *Organization Development Newsletter,* (Fall 1988).

Spradley, James. *The Ethnographic Interview.* New York: Holt, Rinehart and Winston, 1979.

9. Implementing Self-Managed Teams in a Company's Most Productive and Profitable Plant: Why Risk Change?

Patricia V. Averett

Why would a highly successful company risk jeopardizing that success by implementing major organizational change? It would do so only if it determined that the risk of not changing is greater than the risk of change. For some organizations, success masks serious problems lurking just below the surface which threaten to belie that success and eventually erode it. This chapter is about just such an organization. Although it is a manufacturing plant, the dilemmas are universal.

Introduction

The client is a highly successful, non-union manufacturing plant, which is part of a six billion-dollar Fortune 200 company. It is the most profitable and productive plant in a division designated as the *rising star* in the company. The plant is a small one; 50 people total. Thirty-five of them are hourly plant workers. These workers are a stable, highly-experienced workforce. Their average tenure is 16 years with many having worked at the plant for over 20 years. The original plant organizational chart is typical of most small manufacturing plants. (See Figure 1 on the following page.)

This chapter will examine why the decision was made to risk change and transform this plant from a hierarchical structure to self-managed teams. It will also examine what factors influenced the plant manager to overcome his initial resistance to the change effort, and what the transformation has meant to the plant management team, the plant workers, and the organization as a whole. In addition, it will highlight the most critical decisions faced by management and workers during the process. Finally, it will list some of the most significant results achieved through the transformation.

Inception of the Change Process

Historically, management/worker relationships in the plant had generally been very good, but the internal operations had been sloppy. Inside, the plant had always been dirty and the equipment had not been well maintained. Consequently, the company's operations manager hired a new plant manager whose mission was to "shape things up" through

---

Patricia Averett, M.S.O.D., is President of the consulting firm Organization Perspectives, Inc., Box 3206, Annapolis, MD 21403.

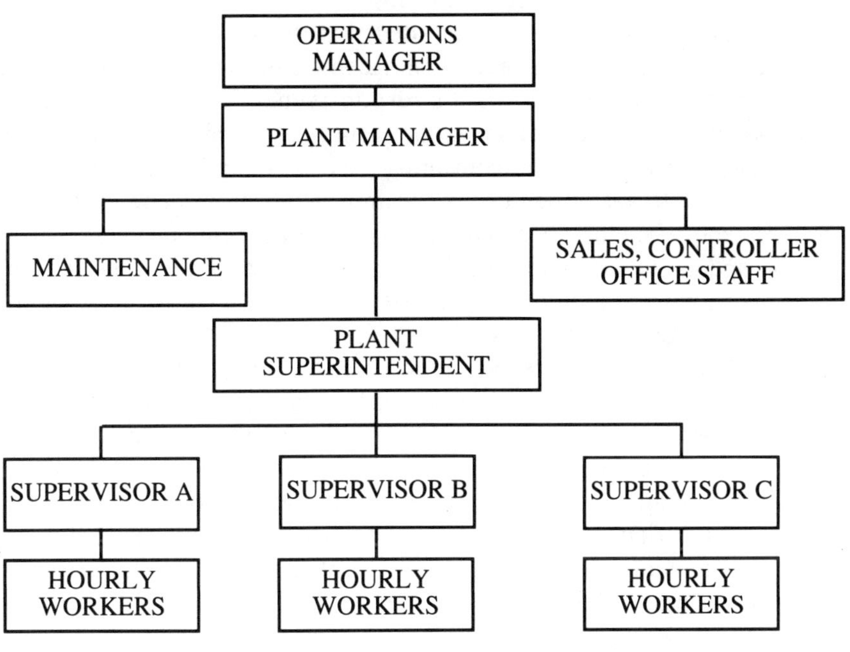

Figure 1: Old Organization Chart

tighter controls. The plant manager did this all too well. He installed new equipment, painted the plant, implemented strict housekeeping policies and procedures, and managed workers through threats of harsh discipline and firing. Grievances began to increase. Whenever the plant workers wanted to appeal a grievance decision through the plant's four-step grievance procedure, they never got past the third step because this step went to the plant manager. He threatened to fire them if they took it further. His first line supervisors also modeled his supervisory style, resulting in frequent confrontations with the hourly workers.

The plant manager was very proud of what he had accomplished over his five-year tenure. His plant was still the most profitable and productive and now, as he put it, "You could eat off the floor." No decision was made without his knowledge and approval. He knew there were some morale problems, but he attributed these to trouble makers and was sure the installation of new equipment and the clean plant would instill pride in the workers and improve morale. Corporate management admired his squeaky clean plant and the profitable results; they never bothered to talk with the plant workers. The operations manager, however, had begun to hear of growing problems between management and workers.

Workers referred to the plant manager as *the warden* and characterized his style as *my way or the highway.* Although no one was ever fired, the frequent threats had their intended effect. Fear permeated the plant, but resentment and anger also began to build.

The operations manager concluded that the strained management/worker relationships would severely threaten the plant's future competitive position by inhibiting the plant's responsiveness to the marketplace. Because of the internal problems, the plant was already demonstrating a great deal of resistance to implementing the corporation's quality improvement process. It was impossible for them to focus on meeting customers' requirements when their own requirements were not being met.

The operations manager thought that a flatter structure with self-managed teams would tap into the workers' expertise and enhance the plant's competitive position by decreasing decision time and increasing initiative, collaboration, and responsiveness at all levels. He believed this plant was a perfect candidate for self-managed teams since it was small and the workers were highly knowledgeable and experienced. Thus, he worked out a plan to *phase in* these changes over the course of one year.

The plant management team, however, saw no need for such sweeping change. As difficult as things were on an interpersonal level, they were otherwise content with the status quo. The plant was successful, and people were secure in their jobs. Why mess with a good thing? They knew that some workers were dissatisfied, but the problems were nothing that a little more control couldn't solve.

The dilemma for the operations manager then became, "Do we risk jeopardizing bottom line results for the sake of improving relationships and the quality of work life? Can we continue to operate like this and be successful? On the other hand, given the fact that the bottom line is so good despite the problems, could it be even better if management/worker relationships improved? And even if profit and productivity were not affected, is the goal of improving relationships and the quality of work life in and of itself a worthy one?

The operations manager weighed the pros and cons and decided that doing nothing would be the greater risk. He could not tolerate the adversarial climate which now existed in the plant, and he could only foresee the problems mushrooming in the future. Although the plant manager opposed the plan for change, the operations manager felt that he would come around once he realized the benefits. The operations manager decided the plan would work and that it was worth taking the risk. The only problem was, he didn't know how to make it happen. He then hired me as a consultant to assist him in the change effort.

Beginning the Intervention

I met with the operations manager and the plant manager several times to discuss how they would proceed. It was clear that the plant manager had reservations about the wisdom of self-managed teams and that he was personally uncomfortable with it. His favorite phrase was, "How can we turn the zoo over to the monkeys?"

Although the operations manager believed the plant manager would eventually support the change, I was unconvinced and knew that we could not proceed without his full commitment and support. It was also clear to me that, while they talked about problems in the plant, no one had clearly defined the issues. The evidence was anecdotal and hearsay. As a first step, I suggested gathering data through personal interviews with the plant management team and a percentage of plant workers to determine the situation. I further stipulated that the data would be fed back to everyone, and some commitment to address major issues would follow. Both the operations manager and the plant manager agreed.

I interviewed the entire plant management team and approximately one-third of the hourly workers. The hourly workers represented all three shifts, all job classifications, and top, middle, and low performers.

Data Uncovers the Real Issues

The data from the management team revealed positive relationships with the plant manager, but no coordination or interdependence among his direct reports. There was, in fact, no team at all: Each manager had a one-on-one relationship with the plant manager. They had never held a staff meeting, and the individual managers saw no reason to communicate with each other on a regular basis.

The data from the plant workers revealed a very different perspective. Deep-seated anger and hostility existed among them toward management; especially the plant manager. A state of *internal warfare* existed, and daily life at the plant was trying for many, at best, and becoming impossible for some. The major issues raised by the workers were lack of involvement in decision making, unresponsive management, lack of respect, lack of communication and information, inconsistent application of plant policies and discipline, and perception of differential treatment. Some direct quotes from the interviews are as follows:

"Morale is at an all time low."

"They should treat the hourly people like human beings."

"This is like army camp."

"Favoritism is big. If you're in the clique, you're OK."

"Supervisors listen, but it goes in one ear and out the other. They don't care."

"Supervisors don't help. Answers aren't there when you need an answer."

"It takes forever to get anything done."

"We never know what's happening."

"I used to do so much extra, now I don't bother."

Decision to Terminate the Process

The data was first fed back to the operations manager. The information was worse than he had thought, but it only served to reinforce his resolve to implement his plan for change. He knew the plant would not remain successful and competitive with such a volatile internal environment.

The data was then fed back to the plant manager, who became visibly upset. His anger at the plant workers was overwhelming. He knew there were some problems and morale was bad, but he never expected the depth of negative emotion that so clearly existed. Seeing the words in black and white and knowing that even his "good workers" felt the same as the others was particularly disturbing to him. As far as he was concerned, he had greatly improved their working environment. He had installed new equipment and the plant was cleaner than ever, yet the workers stabbed him in the back. After all he had done for them, this is what he gets in return? His feedback session ended with him telling me to get out of his office.

According to our agreement, the data was then fed back to the entire plant management team with the operations manager and the plant manager in attendance. The entire team reacted with anger, defensiveness, and denial. They even denied the data from their own interviews that indicated they did not function as a team. For them, the data only served to reinforce their own feelings of acrimony and hostility toward the plant workers. The data revealed emotions and problems that everyone knew existed but which no one had surfaced and discussed.

During the subsequent feedback session to the plant workers, which the operations manager attended, the atmosphere was very different. The data was validated and reinforced by further discussion and clarification. From their point of view, the data depicted what their life was really like at the plant.

How the group behaves during the feedback session is one of the most prescient indicators of the likelihood of success for any OD intervention. Obviously, a major impediment to positive change existed. The extent of denial and the degree of resistance from the plant manager and the management team ultimately told me there was a lot of work to do before they could even embark on such an ambitious process of change. My observations led me to recommend suspension of the project at that time. The operations manager reluctantly accepted the recommendation. I gave him suggestions on what he could do to try to influence the plant manager's thinking over time. As far as I was concerned, however, the project was terminated.

This painful decision created a major dilemma for the operations manager. He was convinced that change was necessary for the survival of the plant, yet he knew the plant manager presented a major block to implementing his plan. He was faced with the choice of giving the plant manager some time to think things through or replacing him with someone whose philosophy was already aligned with his own. He decided to wait.

Growth Process Begins for the Plant Manager

Over the course of the following year, the operations manager continued to work to subtly influence the plant manager to accept the concepts of employee involvement and empowerment. Two pivotal influences on the plant manager occurred during this time: his attendance at a workshop on organizational empowerment (which I had recommended), and his own rising level of discomfort at work. Coming to work every day became stressful and painful for him, just as it was for plant workers. He could no longer ignore the feedback data, nor could he ignore the fact that the plant had serious internal problems which were getting worse. Deep down he knew what the plant workers had said was true. His penchant for control had certainly produced some positive results, but he had gone too far. As he later admitted, "It was no fun to know that when I walked through the plant, workers may say 'hello' to me, but they were thinking, 'I hate your guts'." And because of his own control measures, the most minute decisions took up much of his time (e.g., what color to paint the safety stripes on the plant floor). He had very little time for planning or visiting customers.

The empowerment workshop convinced him there were alternatives to the state of internal warfare which existed at the plant; alternatives which would create empowerment and partnership at all levels and which were completely within his power to implement. He finally admitted that he too wanted things to change. After much deliberation, the plant manager agreed to implement the change outlined by the operations manager with the clear recognition that his own behavior and role, along with those of his management team, would have to drastically change. Thus, 18 months after the initial data gathering process had begun, the operations manager again called on me for assistance.

Change Process Resurrected

Remember that the objectives of the change effort were to internally restructure the plant to enhance its competitive position in the marketplace, maintain its lead position in the '90s and beyond, and resolve problems between management and workers. The changes were to occur in phases. The first phase of the restructuring was to eliminate two levels of management; a senior management position and first line supervision. The second phase called for reorganization into self-managed teams led by hourly crew leaders. The third phase would implement a system for plant-wide employee involvement in decision making.

The operations manager believed his own position was unnecessary and ultimately planned to be promoted, thus eliminating one of the senior levels of plant management. When no promotion materialized, however, he left the organization for a position elsewhere. This left responsibility for the change effort squarely on the shoulders of the plant manager.

While the operations manager's departure could have killed the plan a second time, just the opposite happened. The plant manager now "owned" the process and from then on never wavered in his commitment to, and support of, the process. Also in accordance with the plan, the first line production supervisors were transferred to other positions, thus completing the removal of two management layers. In addition, maintenance was restructured. Now instead of reporting to the plant manager, the group reported to its internal customers. The new organizational chart is illustrated in Figure 2.

Figure 2: New Organization Chart

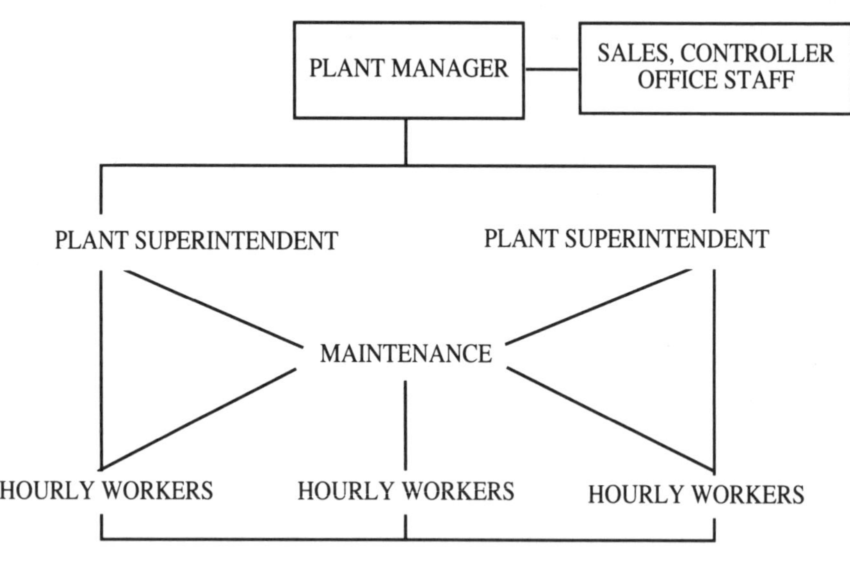

Critical Choices for Management and Workers

Once the organization was restructured, the design of the actual system for employee involvement could begin. During the design phase, several critical choice points arose.

Since I wanted to be sure the management team was truly committed to the undertaking and understood exactly what would be involved before I began working with the plant workers again, I began the intervention with the plant management team. The team consisted of the plant manager, two production superintendents, the director of sales, and the plant controller.

My work with the management team consisted of six, one-day, off-site meetings every other week over a two-and-a-half-month period. The first meeting educated them about empowerment and employee involvement systems through lecture and case study discussion. The next four meetings focused on team development at which time they defined a core mission, clarified and negotiated roles and responsibilities, examined their own decision making and problem solving processes, and defined their objectives for the change process.

Leadership development was the topic of the last meeting. The focus was on building their awareness and skills in the use of influence to achieve results, while minimizing the use of formal authority. Through the use of an assessment-based leadership development instrument, the managers received objective feedback on the effectiveness of their leadership behavior first as individuals and then as a group. The last meeting closed with individual task-oriented action planning to help the team maintain their leadership assets and improve their leadership liabilities relative to the expectations clarified in the team development meetings. At the end of the two-and-a-half months, the team had become more knowledgeable of exactly what the employee involvement process would entail and what changes it would mean for them as a team and as individuals.

The management team reached a critical choice point when it began to realize the scope of the decisions the plant workers would be making under the new system. To ensure they clearly faced this issue, I had the team list all the major categories of decisions management now made, who actually made the decision, and who should make it in the future. From this long list of decisions, the team realized that approximately 50 percent of them could and should be made by plant workers.

This was simultaneously exhilarating and frightening to the management team. Could they actually trust the workers to make such decisions? And what exactly would their new roles be if the workers made all of those decisions? By the end of the process, they understood that for the system to truly be an employee involvement and empowerment system—not merely lip service—they did indeed have to allow the workers to make significant decisions for themselves. They became more comfortable when they understood that employee involvement did not mean abdication of managerial responsibility.

Through team development, they also began to see the need for interdependence among themselves. The production superintendents realized the controller and director of sales made very valuable contributions and vice versa. The plant manager recognized the value of periodically having his entire team together. As a result, the team committed to having regular staff meetings in order to coordinate goals and activities and operate as a cohesive management body.

The outcome of the team development process was a solid commitment to change. They even formally declared a name for the process. Since the operations manager's original plan called for implementation in phases, the process had become known as the "Phase Process" throughout the plant. One of the production superintendents thought that *PHASE* should stand for something, so he made it an acronym which now stands for "Participative Hourly And Salary Empowerment," or P.H.A.S.E.

We set a date for a kick-off meeting for the new P.H.A.S.E. process. The kick-off was held during a three-hour meeting on each shift. During this meeting, we communicated five main pieces of information:

■ Why P.H.A.S.E. had been terminated for 18 months.

■ What the plant manager's original attitudes had been, and why he changed.

■ The management team's new mission statement from its team development sessions.

■ What was going to happen during each phase of the change process.

■ What was expected of everyone, including the plant workers. We also answered questions.

During the following week, I interviewed the plant workers again to gather information about what life was currently like in the plant, and to see if any changes had occurred over the previous 18 months. It was clear that the same issues remained salient for the workers. The only difference was that now they were jaded, cynical, and skeptical of any real change occurring because of the fact that the process was halted 18 months ago when their hopes had been raised. Implementation would clearly be more challenging than it would have been the first time around.

To allow for comparison of before and after conditions, I designed and administered a 30-item survey to all hourly workers. (Excerpts of the results are noted at the end of the chapter.)

We believed it was necessary to educate the workers about how to be a constructive part of participative processes. Therefore, the same empowerment workshop that the operations manager and plant manager had attended was facilitated internally for the entire plant. Shift meetings were held to discuss their applications. During one of these meetings, I had the hourly workers go through the same exercise that management had completed regarding who should make which decisions. The lists made by the management team during team development were almost identical to the plant workers' lists. A Transition Management Team (TMT) comprised of eight hourly workers and three management members was formed to manage the transition and work as liaisons between management and the hourly workers.

Through shift meetings, workers were immediately involved in designing the new system for self-managed teams and employee involvement in decision making. One of the most critical choices they faced during this design phase was whether they needed crew leaders. Along with the removal of first line supervisors, the operations manager's plan had called for the addition of ten hourly crew leaders (two for each shift and two for maintenance) who would be paid slightly higher wages.

I took a more directive stance on this issue, questioning with both the management team and the plant workers whether crew leaders were actually necessary. I feared that crew leaders would become something like supervisors, and the same problems would develop with them that had existed with the first line supervisors.

Some members of the management team were adamant about having crew leaders; at least there would be some "control." Others, including the plant manager, agreed with me. Some hourly workers began to question whether they needed or wanted crew leaders. Those in favor of having crew leaders generally fell into two groups: the workers who thought they would become crew leaders and get extra pay, and those who still wanted to blame someone else for their problems and, thus, needed crew leaders for that purpose. The central question became, "Who makes the decision regarding crew leaders?" Does management make the decision, the hourly workers, or the TMT?

The plant's workforce faced its first major decision under the embryonic P.H.A.S.E. process, and I believed it was one that had to be made by the hourly workers. I advised the management team that if it made the decision, the P.H.A.S.E. process would die before it began. After all, P.H.A.S.E. is about employee involvement in decision making. If management made this decision, it would be completely contradictory to that philosophy. After much debate, the management team agreed the decision had to be made by the plant workers.

For the plant workers, the crew leader decision proved to be a major turning point in the development of their trust in the management team and the participative process. Up until that point, the majority of workers did not believe they were going to be making decisions of any importance. The crew leader decision began to change some attitudes.

The crew leader decision was to be made at a plant-wide meeting of hourly workers. Prior to that meeting, I held shift meetings to prepare them for the decision. Each shift examined the pros and cons of having crew leaders, and workers holding strong opinions on either side of the issue articulated their positions. No voting took place at the shift meetings.

In preparation for the plant-wide meeting, I had also given an assignment to the hourly members of the Transition Management Team. Many of their peers had asked for information about where this type of employee involvement system had been tried before and if it had worked.

In response to their requests, I assigned five case studies to the five pairs of hourly workers on the TMT. The case studies were classics. Some had crew leaders and some did not; some had worked, and some had not. The TMT pairs were to be prepared to present information regarding the situation in their assigned case study (e.g., what was tried, why it worked or did not work, and what the outcome was) to their fellow workers at the plant-wide meeting.

The day of the big meeting arrived. The case study presentations opened the meeting. One pair refused to present their case study; the other four pairs did an outstanding job. They presented the cases with eloquence and clarity and covered all the salient points. The plant workers in the audience had many questions for the case presenters, particularly about what worked or did not work.

The vote was then taken by secret ballot and counted by two hourly workers and me. The outcome was overwhelmingly against having crew leaders; only two workers voted for them. A major decision was made in favor of truly equal self-managed teams, and it was made by the workers themselves. We were now able to move on with designing the P.H.A.S.E. system.

Hourly workers, in cooperation with management, designed the new structure and implemented the support systems necessary to sustain it. The design was based on the issues that the original interviews had surfaced as major needs: plant policy, discipline, unresponsiveness to daily decisions, etc. Through the P.H.A.S.E. process, workers make decisions with their crew teams about their day-to-day work. Workers also now have policy, safety, and human resources committees (comprised of hourly workers with one management advisor) through which they make decisions which were previously the sole purview of management.

For example, the policy committee has completely rewritten the plant policy manual which has been approved by the plant manager. The human resources committee has resolved problems between fellow workers which previously would have resulted in a grievance and possible disciplinary action. When a fellow crew member wants to take a vacation or calls in sick, the crews themselves decide who will cover for the absent worker. As a result, coverage has improved dramatically under the P.H.A.S.E. system.

The production superintendents act as educators, advisors, and coaches to the hourly workers, and occasionally sit in on committee meetings. The TMT continues to exist as the committee which oversees the entire process. Its role is to keep tabs on what is working and what is not, make recommendations for system adjustments and, whenever it is unclear, decide where in the system a particular decision should be made. Figure 3 on the following page illustrates the design, structure, and responsibility of each part of the P.H.A.S.E. system.

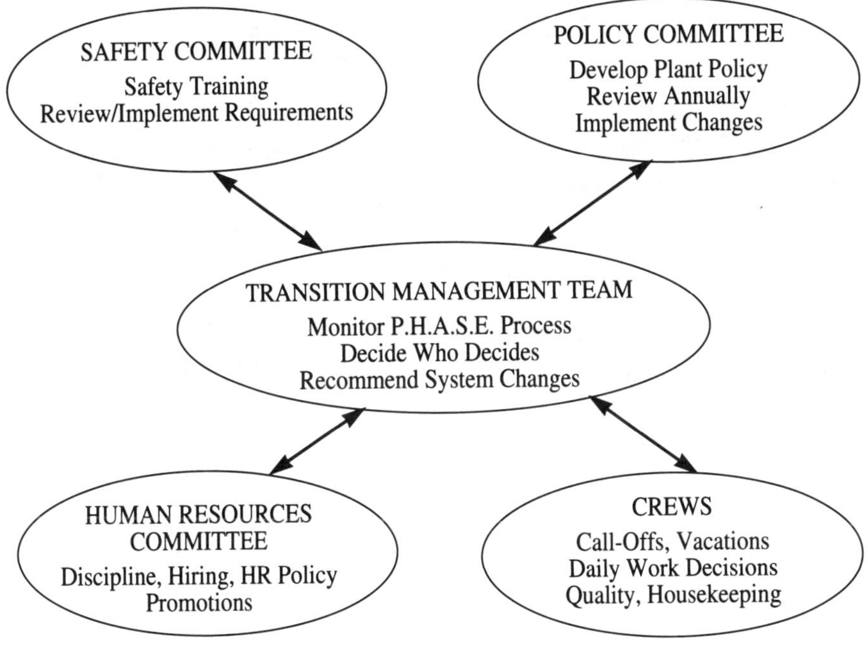

The Results

So what were the results, and was it all worth it? Our survey looked at four main areas:

- Management/Worker Relationships.

- Worker/Worker Relationships.

- How workers felt about working at the plant.

- How workers felt about P.H.A.S.E.

A comparison of the results from the first survey administered in September, 1989, with the identical survey re-administered six months later in March, 1990, when the design process was completed, yields the highlights featured in Table 1 on the following page.

In addition, the bottom line was affected. In comparison with the first quarter of 1989, the first quarter of 1990 showed a 30 percent increase in production and a 45 percent improvement in quality. Downtime due to maintenance dropped by an average of over 600 percent per month. Interestingly, a sister plant right next door is in the midst of a union organizing attempt in which this plant has no interest.

Table 1: Survey Results Comparison

Management/Worker Relationships
Strongly Agree
or Agree

"The plant management team is effective."	Sept. 1989	6%
	Mar. 1990	**40%**
"The management team helps me to do a better job."	Sept. 1989	6%
	Mar. 1990	**40%**

Worker/Worker Relationships

"The level of cooperation among plant workers is low."	Sept. 1989	66%
	Mar. 1990	**38%**
"My shift works well together as a team."	Sept. 1989	52%
	Mar. 1990	**77%**
"My crew is capable of making good decisions together."	Sept. 1989	83%
	Mar. 1990	**92%**

Attitudes Towards Working At the Plant

"Morale is low."	Sept. 1989	97%
	Mar. 1990	**52%**
"If I make a wrong decision I will be punished for it."	Sept. 1989	48%
	Mar. 1990	**9%**

Attitudes Towards the P.H.A.S.E. Process

"The P.H.A.S.E. process will succeed."	Sept. 1989	17%
	Mar. 1990	**52%**
"P.H.A.S.E. is just another management ploy."	Sept. 1989	63%
	Mar. 1990	**42%**

Impact of P.H.A.S.E.

The impact of P.H.A.S.E. goes much further than the documented results are able to show. For example, the plant manager is now one of the biggest advocates of employee involvement. He has become "unburdened." He views his role as one of shaping the environment and overseeing plant operations on a global scale. Rather than become involved in every decision, he is able to spend more time planning and traveling with his director of sales to meet with customers. They have even taken some hourly employees to meet with customers. And the company has also given the plant manager responsibility for a second plant. He is planning to implement an employee involvement system in this plant as well.

The production superintendents have benefited also. They no longer work a harried 65-hour week. They now work 40-45 hours and rarely go in on weekends. They carry beepers for emergencies but rarely have to use them. Their life at the plant has been transformed. Instead of stressful, adversarial relationships with plant workers, they operate mostly in an advisory capacity, sitting in on committee meetings and making sure the workers have all the information they need to do their jobs and make appropriate decisions.

The workers no longer depend on management to get things done for them. They have taken charge of their lives at the plant and have realized that their individual and collective contributions make a significant difference. For example, when the plant was expanding its facilities, the maintenance crew researched different lighting alternatives on their own and decided to install new fixtures which gave more light yet used significantly less electricity. Even workers who have been reluctant to actively participate are beginning to volunteer for the policy, safety, or human resources committees when it becomes time for members to rotate.

In summary, P.H.A.S.E. has helped this plant build relationships and trust which have enabled everyone to use their expertise and perform to the best of their ability. Together they have overcome barriers which eventually would have compromised the future success of the plant.

10. Esso's New Directions: Review of a Major Organisational Effectiveness Intervention

Clyde McMillan

Esso Australia Ltd. (EAL), an affiliate of Exxon Corporation, is responsible for the corporation's oil and gas activity in Australia, producing and processing crude oil and gas from 13 offshore platforms in Bass Strait. This operation, employing 1,300 people, produces 450 million cubic feet of gas and 350,000 barrels of crude oil daily. This represented 62 percent of the total Australian crude oil demand in 1988 and contributed a credit of A$2.7 billion against its trade deficit of A$15 billion that year.

Since 1985, the fundamental challenge of the production department has become one of changing from an expanding operation to an operation in the mature phase of declining production. New discoveries of comparable size to the fields then in production were unlikely, so the company had to reduce costs to make smaller fields viable. The corporation then set out to achieve two strategic goals in Australia: to make the most effective use of remaining hydrocarbon resources in Bass Strait, and to position EAL to take opportunities for expanding its resource base in predominantly smaller fields throughout Australia by both acquisition and development.

Several studies of manpower and operations examined how the company should conduct operations during the coming years of declining production. It became clear that to achieve its two strategic goals, EAL's modus operandi had to change. Some of the change issues for its people to consider were as follows.

■ There was a need for the highest level of employee business skills.

■ The company needed to be able to respond quickly to opportunities in the marketplace and bring discoveries to production.

■ Creative, low-cost solutions needed to be identified and developed. Access to the best technology was crucial.

■ Work practices needed to be changed where they constrained the realisation of the full potential of the people involved.

■ Less employee supervision was needed, but more leadership was essential.

Change Programme

In 1986 EAL began a two-year change programme. The programme began with workshops that resulted in the establishment of task forces

Clyde McMillan is with Exxon Chemicals Australia, Ltd., Private Mailbag No. 3, Altona, Vic. 3018, Australia.

that developed plans to identify and solve crucial issues and change attitudes. Results included a "vision for the future" and some significant changes in management style and corporate culture, including increased delegation, changes to leadership styles, senior manager support for change, a changed attitude towards mistakes, and less paperwork. These are discussed more fully later in the chapter.

The workshops took a look at the functional, highly-structured organisation that existed and set out to define an ideal organisation. This involved visualising the "future look" of the organisation in the context of what its role might be in 1995. The aim was to draw on the experiences of EAL's people to develop ideas about how to achieve high performance. The workshops' designers and the production manager were looking beyond the workshops, hoping that they would empower line managers to identify, experiment with, and implement changes.

The "New Directions" workshops were conducted in the Production Department only—not corporate-wide. Therefore, right from the beginning, there were obstacles and resistance to change as the programme progressed because the rest of the company was involved only as interested observers. In 1989 hindsight, embarking upon large scale changes in a single department was a critical variable to the subsequent success of "New Directions" because several key corporate-wide decisions were made in 1988 which had a negative impact on the "New Directions" programme.

Change activities were also taking place elsewhere in Exxon. For example, affiliates such as Esso Resources Canada and Exxon Chemicals had made significant changes within the previous two years. The experiences of these companies were reviewed when establishing the conceptual bases for the "New Directions" programme. A chronological summary of the change programme follows.

1984–'85	Organisational Reviews
1986	"New Directions" Workshops for the
	Production Department
	Vision of the Future Validated
1987–'88	Task Forces Tackle Key Issues
	Changes Implemented

Conceptual Bases of "New Directions"

The "New Directions" activity was planned and implemented by a four-member team, including a senior line manager, a training and development specialist, an OD specialist, and a management consultant. The team reported to, and had the support of, the General Manager (GM) of Production. Indeed he was the programme's key sponsor.

Organisational Cultures

The first four workshops used Deal and Kennedy's (1982) model of culture as a basis for developing a picture of the existing EAL culture. Participants were asked to describe the culture in terms of heroes, values, cultural networks, and rites and rituals, and then identify any mixed messages. The resultant picture showed a culture which was one of "over protection/dependence." This type of culture clearly was inconsistent with that needed for the organisation to achieve its goals in the operating environment of 1986.

The culture exercise focused the group's attention on the existing organisation, setting the scene to develop a "vision" of the desired organisation.

The Vision

Following Waterman's (1980) proposition that "structure is not organisation," participants were asked to define, in terms of the McKinsey 7S Model (Waterman, et. al., 1980), the organisation they would like to be part of in 1995. The 7S Model is shown in Figure 1.

Figure 1: McKinsey's "7S" Model

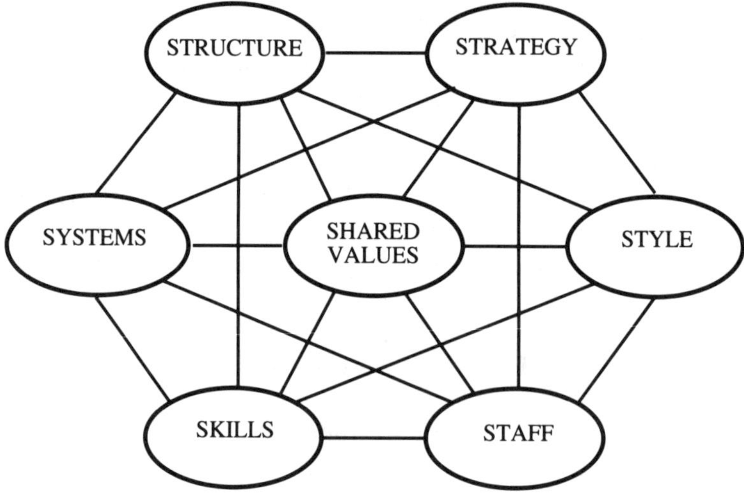

Direction of each "S" should be consistent with all other "S's" and corporate mission.

Waterman (1982) had described the 7S Model as "seven elements of strategic fit" whose alignment with each other was necessary for an effective organisation. He drew an analogy between the alignment of compasses in a magnetic field. We wanted our vision, mission statement, objectives, culture, and organisational process to all be aligned.

By developing a vision for 1995, we hoped to obviate people's inclination merely to extrapolate from 1986. The aim was to visualise the ideal organisation, and then work on how to achieve that ideal. The question posed was this: "It is 1995, and you are there. What sort of organisation (Production Department) do you see? Describe it in terms of the 7S Model."

The results of this activity were excellent. A vision of the future was produced and part of this is shown in Figure 2.

Figure 2: Vision of the Future

Strategy

- Change—seen as way of life/look to improve performance/challenge constraints
- New business opportunities—actively seek/ respond quickly and effectively to
- Technology—stay at leading edge, exploit information technology
- Employees — committed to shared values

Staff

- High achievers/creative, innovative entrepreneurial/flexible, satisfied/well rewarded
- Management and professional career streams recognized
- Experience outside normal area of expertise
- People-oriented managers
- Experience
- Remuneration based on contribution
- Most suitable people recruited at all levels
- High investment in training and development

Structure

- Flat organization
- Self-supporting operating groups
- Task force project development groups
- Mentor role provided for

Shared Values

- Energy for Australia— profit for the company and its people
- People are our prime asset
- Trust, openness, candor, teamwork, mutual support
- Rewards for contribution valued
- Innovation
- Safe work place
- High ethical standards

Skills

- Technical competence/ computer skilled
- All round managers/ leadership/change management
- Innovation, entrepreneurship/commercial acumen
- Multi-skilled, flexible, versatile
- Excellent communication
- Good skill assessment techniques
- Effective contractor/ consultants

Systems

- Performance assessment, career planning—fair and motivating
- Control systems are simple, the minimum necessary
- Contracting system is simple
- Program for maintenanc of safe and healthy work place
- All systems based on maximum delegation of authority
- Computer systems are user driven and friendly

Style

- High commitment to company's values/few controls/trusting
- Innovation encouraged/ guidelines not policy manuals, mistakes tolerated
- Open, informal communications/participative decision-making
- Responsibility, authority down the line
- Managers are leaders, approachable, non-punitive, supportive
- Esso people seen as dynamic, purposeful, result-oriented, practical, business-like, competent, flexible, versatile, "fleet-footed," high integrity

Participants were enthusiastic about what they had produced and keen to get on with achieving the vision. Indeed 1995 seemed too far away—why not do it by 1987!

The picture painted by participants of the 1995 organisation was only the first step. The final product, of course, had to be acceptable to and *owned* by all of the company's workforce. Therein lay the key challenge. Each work group generated its own visions. The resulting 70 or so were remarkably similar to the basic model developed by the first four workshops. The key point, however, was that at the conclusion of these workshops, the company had a vision that everyone *owned.*

Individual Responsibility for Making a Difference

In any large organisation, the responsibility for change rests with people at all levels. (See Figure 3.)

Figure 3: The Shared Responsibility for Change

TOP MANAGEMENT	1	POLICIES/VALUES
MIDDLE MANAGEMENT	2	TONE/APPROACH
ORGANISATIONAL UNITS	3	ACTION/ACHIEVEMENT

Top management's responsibility is to identify the need for and then define and communicate values, philosophies, and policies. Middle management's responsibility is to broadly interpret, amplify, and reinforce these values, philosophies, and policies, and then set the tone and approach to be followed by each organisational unit. The organisational units are charged with responsibility of taking action based on their own initiative plus guidelines from middle and top management.

When planning the workshops, middle management was identified as having a key role in facilitating organisational change. As the model in Figure 3 shows, middle managers interface with both top management and the organisational units. Consequently, the initial workshops were targeted at this group of approximately 120 people. Subsequent workshops were aimed at "communicating the vision" and allowing all employees to participate in the process, thus becoming *owners* of the outcome. The first round of four workshops involved about 60 middle managers. The "vision for the future" was developed in these early workshops. Furthermore, some critical change issues were identified. The process resulted in a remarkable level of consistency from one workshop to the next.

Workshop participants were encouraged to undertake change on a personal level in their work groups. The collation of participants' plans for personal change was an important feature of the workshop follow-up activity. This information was circulated so that people could identify others with similar objectives.

People left the workshops with both a personal change agenda and one for their work groups. The workshops had succeeded in stimulating middle managers to be the initiators of change.

The format for the next three workshops, attended by the remainder of the middle management, was changed to work on the following items: a review of the vision, review of the change issues, suggested changes to the vision and/or the change issues, and the next steps.

At the end of these workshops, middle management was committed to the vision and supported the changes needed. The workshops thereafter set out to communicate the vision in an open-minded fashion. The "vision" became a dynamic concept: It could be challenged, changed, and enhanced progressively in the light of the suggestions made at the workshops. The workshops succeeded in generating a high level of commitment to change throughout the department. So much so, in fact, that one of the significant challenges at the end of the process was the pressure to bring 1995 forward to tomorrow. These workshops had generated over 1,000 ideas for incorporation into the plans for change.

Outcomes of the Workshop Process

At the end of the workshop process, a composite "vision of the future" was collated and published throughout the department. This is shown in Figure 2. The workshops created an environment where people saw it as their responsibility to *make change happen*. Some of the more notable characteristics of this new environment were:

■ Senior management was seen as actively supporting change.

■ Increased delegation and acceptance of a less formal presentation style for developing change initiatives and day-to-day business decision making.

■ A new leadership style was identified: Managers manage people. People manage tasks.

■ A commitment to reduce paperwork and look more critically for value-added initiatives in review processes.

■ A culture change relating to mistakes and risk taking, provided that the highest standards of integrity were upheld in the areas of safety and ethics.

■ Increased focus on customer and client relationships in the organisation.

These factors lead to a series of change management "experiments" at both the individual and group or division levels throughout the organisation. Following the communication of the vision, task forces were formed to develop concepts identified as critical during the workshops. Figure 4 lists the critical issues and shows their relation to the McKinsey model.

Figure 4: The 7S Model Critical Change Times

Managing the Change

A management steering committee appointed task force leaders who sought the input of individuals interested in the task subject. Typically, this was done by publicising the activity and asking for volunteers to join the task forces.

Task force activities brought people together from diverse work locations and backgrounds which, in itself, served to increase awareness of the value of collaborative work practices and cooperation (key elements of the vision). For the purpose of illustration, some experiments and task force activities are described below.

Waterman (1982) posited that in addition to structure, an organisation has six other complementary elements — style, strategy, staff, skills, shared values, and systems. Nonetheless, immediately following the visioning workshops, two experiments in organisational structure were initiated, seemingly ignoring the vision which had been developed. The vision's reference to "self-supporting operating groups" and "flatter" organisational structure (with fewer supervisors) clearly implied change in the structure which had previously been organised on functional or discipline lines (e.g., Civil Design, Process Engineering, Accounting, Administration, and so on).

The two experiments in organisational structure were run independently of each other; one in the offshore engineering support area and the other at the Longford Plant.

Experiment in Structure — The "E" Team

An experiment called the "E" team was set up to try out the concept of a multi-disciplined team providing the full range of technical support to an offshore operating group — namely the four offshore platforms which made up the Eastern Block. The "E" team consisted of five engineers, a secretary, and a supervisor. They worked alongside the existing organisation and took charge of all technical activities on these platforms.

This experiment was successful. Although it focused on only one facet of change—structure—it worked because the team designed its "modus operandi" around all seven S's.

The "E" team confronted all issues with mixed success. The success of the experiment was embodied in the subsequent restructuring of the Gippsland Technical Division, which set up similarly self-sufficient Block Support teams backed by a number of specialist groups. This organisation is now regarded as essential to the effective operation of the offshore platforms.

Experiment in Structure—The Longford Pilot

Another experiment in organisational structure was initiated at the Longford Plant site, on a much larger and more formal scale than had been attempted in the "E" team. The organisation associated with the operation of the three gas plants and the crude stabilisation plant at Longford was investigated by a task force and thereafter formally restructured to achieve a greater level of autonomy and real accountability in decision making in the plant management.

The Engineering, Accounting, and Administration functions involved in the day-to-day operation of the plants were integrated into the organisation and reported to the plant manager. Specialist support functions needed on an infrequent basis typically remained outside of the plant organisation. The Longford pilot was reviewed during the first quarter of 1989, and the structure was permanently established. Hence, the experiment was successful, and its implementation has enhanced the business effectiveness of the Longford Gas Plant.

Lessons from the Structure Experiments

These experiments illustrated the value of a change in structure in terms of:

■ High levels of support from the Operations people for the "close to the customer" approach.

■ Operations and technical priorities being more consistent.

■ More consistent upward reporting: Elimination of duplicate information paths.

■ Both experiments were independently cited in separate safety audits as a major improvement to effective safety in the field.

■ A higher level of commitment and cooperation between operations and technical people. This manifested itself by technical recommendations being cited as being more consistently practical.

■ An increase in the level of operator innovations. At Longford the "coin your idea" incentive scheme saw a marked increase in submissions (to the order of a three-fold increase).

■ The need for specialists to provide support for multi-discipline teams.

Secretarial Working Group

During "New Directions," the Gippsland secretarial staff became concerned with the need to change its traditional role to keep pace with new technology and organisational changes. A secretarial working group was formed to focus on the new technology, identify the issues, and challenge the secretaries to take a leading role in developing the changes needed. A core group of secretaries reporting to management was formed and given responsibility to develop job classification and job profiles, individual career paths, training, and mentoring.

Action has been taken on all of these issues and has significantly improved the morale and motivation of the secretaries, encouraging them to see their role in broader and more flexible terms. The working group remains an adaptive mechanism for future opportunities. It continues to be a forum for action on current and emerging issues for secretarial staff in Gippsland and a vehicle for seeking input from secretaries on key issues.

Mentor/Specialist Task Force

The workshops identified two key supervisory roles:

■ Mentor: Someone who provides support and guidance to a protege.

■ Specialist: Recognised expert, who provides authoritative advice in a particular field relevant to the business need.

The mentor role was intended to add value to the role of the supervisor by reducing the protege's reliance on a single relationship. The value-added concept for the mentor to be complementary to the supervisor came from the realisation that an additional relationship was the key to overcoming the perceived problem of meeting employee coaching and counseling needs with fewer supervisors. The mentor/protege relationship was seen as being based on friendship. Indeed it was for this reason that the task force recommended that mentors should not take part in the formal appraisal cycle for their proteges. It was felt that the nonthreatening mentor would be a valuable complement to the supervisor in developing people in the company.

The role of the specialist is really one of advisor to the *task managers*. This was consistent with the need identified in the "E" team quality control procedure for managing risks. Continuity of experience was seen as important in the career paths for specialists. Furthermore, specialists in technical areas were envisaged as being more effective where they were part of an active network with individuals who had similar roles in affiliate companies and outside the company.

These roles were seen as having motivational and developmental value, as well as the more obvious service benefits to the organisation. This is supported by literature on mentoring and is, more particularly, illustrated by Dalton's and Thompson's (1986) four stages of career model.

The specialist role has been readily accepted throughout the Production Department. This is exhibited by the way it has been incorporated into the thinking at Longford, in the Technical Division, and in manpower planning. There also has been progress in establishing networks both with Exxon affiliates overseas and also outside the company.

Changes Offshore

The Producing Operations Division is responsible for the offshore operations on the 13 platforms. This division's activities are in the forefront of implementing change with the involvement and cooperation of the trade unions.

Following the vision communication workshops at all locations, the Production Department focused on a coordinated plan of change through work group meetings. The work groups complied a list of 284 items for the department to address. A Change Coordination Group was formed with representation from management, unions, and the workforce. The unions endorsed the concept of "New Directions" with formal resolutions at a local level after seeking information during a number of briefings and discussions on the intended outcomes. This was an important factor for being able to make progress in the process of involving the people.

Initially the Change Coordination Group consisted of 12 people and this settled at five in mid-1988. Concurrent with the mid-1988 change, a full-time change coordinator was appointed to supervise the various change programmes.

"New Directions" has achieved some significant results:

■ Changes to offshore catering to provide "healthy lifestyle" food options.

■ Creation of a promotions development panel to select people for promotion.

■ Planning of career opportunities for non-degreed people.

■ Development of a personnel data base.

■ Restructuring and efficiency discussions with unions.

These and many other projects reflected an increasing involvement and participation of a growing proportion of the offshore workforce.

Since January 1988, the emphasis has moved from the job list of 284 items to facilitating change where the change is felt most. That is to say that the role of the Change Coordination Group has shifted to a facilitating role (i.e., helping those who have identified needed change to implement it).

This mindset has facilitated recent discussions/negotiations with offshore unions on job restructuring. In fact, the restructuring negotiations have seen a more participative style used to gain good results and have enabled the offshore group to be ahead of other groups in this matter.

The most lasting legacy of "New Directions" in the offshore workplace has been the principle of employee participation. The most significant lessons learned offshore about employee participation have been that participation creates expectations and that these expectations must be managed. Finally, when adopting a participative style, management needs to be specific about the limits on the group's recommendations and be prepared to act on the group's recommendations.

"New Directions" Return on Investment

Employee involvement has been heavy in the workshops and subsequent task force activities. By the end of June 1987, about 2,773 man-days (estimated to be about 13 man years or approximately two percent of that period's available manpower) had been devoted to "New Directions" activities. At that time, a task force reviewed the return on effort invested by using the structured interview technique to gather the data. The sample included 50 hourly-wage workers from offshore, Longford, LIP and Barry Beach, 20 engineers, and all managers. Positive outcomes were generally recognised, and there was a high degree of commitment to the vision and its value. For example, the benefits of the new work environment were consistently cited in terms of enhanced productivity resulting from increased delegation, improved morale, and greater cooperation between groups. Over 40 specific examples were reported.

Comments made during the interviews demonstrated that employees had developed high expectations of the change outcomes, some of which were overly optimistic. The target date of 1995 had translated in many people's minds to "tomorrow." Criticisms included lack of action, barriers to change, and an apparent lack of tangible output from the task forces then in progress. Many employees expected only high profile, tangible benefits.

The task forces had been expected to better define the issues and generate realistic plans. On reflection, the parameters within which the task forces were to work could have been defined more clearly. Each virtually had global terms of reference, and it was this unrestrained approach combined with a sudden workload increase that contributed to much workforce frustration. The list without defined plans continued to grow.

The frustrations may have been exacerbated by the coincidental increase in engineering activity following the Government's announcement of some concessions on crude oil excise. This inhibited the ability of the organisation to progress change with the same level of participation.

It was evident that leadership in managing peoples' expectation for change was needed to overcome the sense that the whole process was simply absorbing resources. In response, the task forces were encouraged to draw their conclusions as soon as was practical, and the management steering committee focused on consolidating the gains that had been made.

In evaluating the effort, a shortcoming was the absence of a plan to measure the bottom line effect of the changes which had been made. A clear fix was obtained on the workforce's perception of the impact of changes. However, the missing piece was the measurement of effect on bottom line. The difficulty and challenge of this step is eloquently presented by Lippitt, et. al. (1985). In any other major project, this would have been a key step and requirement.

Despite union support for "New Directions" involvement, which was given guardedly, the survey also highlighted significant resistance from people concerned over the potential undermining of union positions and the implications for job security.

Some of the key lessons in managing change activities which were inferred from the evaluation data included the following:

■ "No" is an acceptable management response to issues raised.

■ It is easy to create high expectations of change but difficult to manage these expectations.

■ For the non-committed, perceived lack of results (when benefits are intangible) will be sufficient to reinforce their opinion that nothing would happen anyway.

■ Flatter organisation will be interpreted as a lessening of opportunity and job security, therefore creating additional barriers to the implementation of change.

■ The level of consensus which is sought on issues needs to be carefully considered and managed— does everything require consensus before action is taken?

■ When people are asked for ideas, they expect quick action from management, even if that action is merely saying, "No."

■ Only key, achievable, and relevant issues should be worked.

■ Personal responsibility for achieving results cannot be stressed enough. There are too many people looking for someone else to take the initiative and direct the change process.

■ Some people, particularly hourly-wage workers, do not want to contribute ideas for change. They expect management to do this.

■ Actions for change must be consistent with business goals and must have a bottom line impact.

What Could Have Been Done Differently?

It is crucial in the human relations development process to learn from experience and evaluate actions and outcomes to see what went well, what didn't, and how the process can be improved to increase performance. These observations may benefit both EAL and others who are embarking on large scale organisational change initiatives.

Change Manager

The management of change was a full-time job in itself as events turned out. Appointment of a senior person as the change manager would have had two positive effects on the workforce:

■ It would have been symbolic of the importance attached to the exercise.

■ He/she would have been a resource to maintain the momentum which built up as a result of the workshop and task forces.

Any other large project would have had a designated leader. As events unfolded, the change activities became decentralized to each line function. While the management steering committee attempted to centralize coordination of a diverse range of activities, a single point of day-to-day contact was needed to pull everything together.

Senior Manager Transfers

Looking back, it would have been ideal not to have changed senior line managers before the programme had developed a critical mass. Some issues associated with transfer of senior people during a change programme are:

■ The new person does not *own* the programme, no matter how sincere his/her intentions.

■ Transfers are a fact of life in a large corporation, so we need to be able to cope with them and develop strategies for handling a management change at any time during the change programme.

■ Some transfers are unavoidable; however, this is another good reason for having a senior change manager in charge of the programme.

The original team facilitators and designers of the programme were also transferred during 1988. This removed a big chunk of enthusiasm and knowledge of the origins and development of the processes then being translated into actions.

In 1989 the production manager was transferred from Australia, removing the major driving force behind the programme.

Training Line Managers as Change Agents

Not enough time was invested in training line managers as change agents. Much of the change was expected to occur in the line organisations, and more time could have been invested in training line managers how to facilitate and manage change.

A particular training emphasis would be on managing expectations and the need to effectively manage change experiments and interventions. Line managers also need well developed facilitation skills. A concern and frustration identified by the evaluation task force was that we tried to do too much too quickly (i.e., the "why wait until 1995" approach). When excise conditions changed in 1987 and less resources were available to maintain the change programme's momentum, the stated targets of task force activities and other "New Directions" activities were not altered.

Bottom Line Effects

An accurate measurement of peoples' perceptions of the results of the workshops and programme was obtained. We knew quite clearly what the intangible results were and, to a lesser extent, what the bottom line results were.

A complementary step was needed—that of developing a plan or strategy for measuring bottom line effects of the changes (i.e., the gathering of what Lippitt, et. al. (1985) referred to as *hard data)*. The difficulty of obtaining hard data on results of organisational change efforts is well described by both Lippitt et. al. (1985) and James and Oliver (1981). In this case, a majority of the data was *soft* (i.e., attitudinal and perceptual) with the minority being *hard data* (i.e., quantitative measures of job and system performance).

Any future activity should devote equal time and effort to developing strategies for gathering both soft and hard data on results.

Overall, the "New Directions" initiative was a success. It is true to say that some change would have taken place anyway, and that the process had come to incorporate all change initiatives under its banner. The key factor here is not the true origins of change, but that "New Directions" offered a legitimate way of celebrating changes. The enhanced pace and extent of change, particularly in 1987, unsurpassed in previous years, illustrates the value of the "New Directions" process.

Challenges for Change Managers

This case study demonstrates the importance of several factors in initiating and sustaining change in culture and attitudes. In algebraic terms, change will occur when resistance to change is exceeded by the combination of:

- The ability to make a difference.
- Overall employee dissatisfaction.
- Availability of resources.
- Development of programme priorities and first steps.

Ability to make a difference is a factor that leaders can bestow. The workshops set out to empower people to take charge of their destiny. The challenge for leaders is to manage the risks involved in establishing mutual trust (i.e., to bestow power and use it responsibly). Ackoff (1972) has challenged us to design adaptive organisations that solve problems interactively, not independently.

A seemingly inescapable conclusion for enterprises facing increasingly rapid changes is that ways need to be found for the empowering process to be ongoing rather than a one-time event. The value in this is not that the outcome should be more logical, but rather that it will be pursued with more vigor and commitment.

Management cannot stand back from the arena of change. All levels must give direction to the change. People's dreams and visions have to be tempered with the reality of the corporation's business plan and goals. It is in this reconciliation of visions with business reality where managers must give leadership and guidance.

Dissatisfaction alone is not enough to result in change. It is often tolerated. This case study has shown that it is linked to expectations. Change managers must manage expectations, set priorities, and communicate to ensure that people do not become dissatisfied with the change process itself. The communication of gains in this case study was not effective in eliminating critical comments during the evaluation of effort. People involved in the day-to-day issues were typically critical of the lack of progress, even where a significant gain had been made only a short time before. This highlights a crucial challenge in managing expectations; namely, ensuring that the gains are recognised in the context of a realistic plan.

The final challenge illustrated was that of resource management. Significant gains in productivity resulted during the programme and were absorbed by a combination of increase in development activity and by transfers out of Gippsland to other operations. These demands on the Gippsland manpower resource inhibited the extent to which the programme could proceed at the same pace as it had started, and may have contributed to the frustration. Change managers must seek a balance between taking full advantage of gains in productivity and providing sufficient surplus resource to sustain continued pursuit of productive change.

Conclusions

From this case study we have concluded that:

■ Participative change processes are powerful tools for establishing the real responsibilities of the individuals as stakeholders for the well-being of the enterprise.

■ Trust and ownership are key factors in the success of the change activity.

■ The organisation had the capacity to identify change issues from within its own resources.

■ By contrast it did not have, nor did it need, the capacity to measure comparative change benefits in a rigorous fashion. Self-supporting operating groups and multi-disciplined technical teams were found to be highly effective.

■ Flatter organisation and multi-disciplined teams set new challenges for career development and the process of managing quality.

■ Managing expectations, ensuring that gains are seen in perspective, and focusing on priorities are fundamental to sustaining a participative change process.

■ Strong leadership and quick action on the issues generated by the process is essential to sustaining participative change. "No" is a legitimate response from management.

■ A major organisational change effort requires a full-time manager or leader.

■ Employees' visions of the future of the organisation must be tempered with business realities.

References

Ackoff, Russell L. *The Second Industrial Revolution.* Wharton School of Finance and Commerce: University of Pennsylvania, 1972.

Clutterbuck, D. *Everyone Needs a Mentor.* London: The Institute of Personnel Management, 1985.

Dalton, G.W. and Thompson, P.H. *Novations.* Glenview, Illinois: Scott Foresman and Company, 1986.

Deal, T.E. and Kennedy, A.A. *Corporate Cultures.* Reading, Massachusetts: Addison-Wesley Publishing Company, 1982.

James, U.S. and Oliver, L.W. *A Preliminary Assessment of the Impact of the Army's Organisational Effectiveness (OE) Programme.* Alexandria, Virginia: Army Research Institute for the Behavioural Sciences, 1981.

Hax, A.C. and Majluf, N.S. "Organisation Design: A Case Study on Matching Strategy and Structure," *Journal of Business Strategy,* (Fall Edition, 1983).

Hayes, J.J. "Esso's Approach to Safety in Plant Design, Testing, and Process Equipment Modifications," *Proceedings of the 1988 Chemical Conference,* Sydney, Australia.

Lippitt, G.L., Langseth, P., and Mossop, J. *Implementing Organisational Change.* London: Jossey-Bass, 1985.

Peters, T. and Waterman, R.H. *In Search of Excellence.* New York: Harper & Row, 1982.

Peters, T. and Austin, N. A Passion for Excellence. New York: Random House, 1985.

Waterman, R.H., Jr., Peters, T., and Phillips, J.R. "Structure is Not Organisation," *Business Horizon,* (June 1980).

Waterman, R.H. "Strategic Organisation: The Seven Elements of Strategic Fit," *The Journal of Business Strategy,* (Winter 1982).

Watson, C.M. "Leadership, Management and the Seven Keys." *McKinsey Quarterly,* (August 1983).

Zey, M.G. *The Mentor Connection.* New York: Dow Jones-Irwin, 1984.

Part Four: Emerging Issues in OD

11. Insights on International Management and Organization Development: Interview With Nancy Adler

Beverly A. Battaglia

Nancy J. Adler is Professor of Organizational Behavior and Cross-Cultural Management at McGill University, 1001 Sherbrook St. West, Montreal, PQ, Canada H3A1G5.

In addition to becoming the first female full professor in the Management faculty at McGill University in Montreal, Canada, Adler is a well-known author and consultant in the international field. Dr. Adler has made substantial contributions to increasing our understanding of cross-cultural management and international organizational behavior.

In 1990, she received the American Society for Training and Development's International Leadership Award. In this interview, Professor Adler shares her current thinking about cross-cultural management and organization development.

Battaglia: How long have you been interested in cross-cultural management and international organizational behavior, and how did you get interested in this area?

Adler: I have probably been interested in the cross-cultural part of cross-cultural management since childhood. What ultimately became my professional focus did not begin to emerge until I was in UCLA's MBA program. In this program, I was specializing in the management of the arts—ballet, theater, music—and had the opportunity to do an internship with the Israeli Minister of Culture.

I went to Israel unable to speak or read a word of Hebrew, and was told by everybody that it wouldn't make any difference because most people with whom I would have contact spoke English. While that may be true, Israelis conduct their meetings in Hebrew. So I arrived knowing no one, met the Minister of Culture on day one, and on day two, she placed me in a Ulpan, the Hebrew language program for new immigrants. That was my first real experience with what I later learned was cultural shock; though at that point it did not have a name—just a reality. I remember writing my mother that I felt like I was in a tumble dryer with a window looking out at the world.

About three months into my internship in 1973, the Yom Kippur War broke out. Here I was a "sunny Southern California kid," who had never

Beverly Battaglia, Ph.D., is President of the management consulting firm Battaglia, Ltd., 2237 N. Westwood Ave., Santa Ana, CA 92706.

expected reality to be worse than not having sunshine on the day I wanted to go to the beach. And here I was in a war.

I returned in 1974 and, much to my disappointment, realized that one of many Americans' main concerns was how long they had to wait in line at gas stations, and how their lives were being inconvenienced by the "energy crisis." By contrast, in Israel the question had been, "Are we going to survive?"

I was also struck by the fact that the Israelis did not appear to feel or express the kind of animosities towards the Arabs that I heard talked about in North America. The focus and value differences between the two countries were striking. After my return, I did not seem to fit back in very well. When you move from people making life and death decisions to people in their second year of an MBA program complaining about how Accounting is not being held at a convenient time, it scrambles your sense of reality a bit. What I was experiencing was reentry shock; but again, I had no word for it.

It wasn't until three months later when I happened to dine with a close friend who had just returned from a Peace Corps assignment in India, that it became clear—both of us were experiencing exactly the same thing. What I had attributed to being in Israel during a war, and the personal experiences I had, were a part of the experience of having gone away, changing, seeing the world in a different way, and then trying to come back to your home country. I was experiencing the same feelings and questioning in returning from Israel that my friend was experiencing in returning from India.

At that time, because of the questions I was asking about my own return, I was invited to meet with returning Peace Corps volunteers. The insights that came from those meetings assisted me in my personal reentry as well as in beginning to understand the overall reentry phenomenon.

I began to look at what was known about reentry. At that point, there was very little. There was some work on cultural shock and cross-cultural adaptation when moving into a foreign culture, but nothing on coming home. My questions ultimately led to my dissertation on reentry of North Americans who had worked all over the world and returned to the United States and Canada.

Last December, I received a call from *The Wall Street Journal* asking about reentry because they were writing an article and wanted to know more about my research. Although the dissertation research is now approximately ten years old, it is a relevant topic for publication today. Perhaps my questions were a little bit ahead of their time.

Battaglia: Originally you focused on reentry issues. Where did you go from there?

Adler: From reentry, my work expanded in a number of areas. I looked more broadly at transition issues, expatriation out to a foreign country, and reentry back home. Then I began to ask, "What are expatriate managers doing while they are abroad?" I began asking a set of questions about what makes an effective manager in a foreign culture. That was the beginning of what I would call cross-cultural management. I started researching cross-cultural negotiations, team building, ways of developing cultural synergy as a form of organizational development, as well as a whole set of management issues viewed from a multinational perspective.

During the last three or four years, I became concerned that all of these individual aspects of cross-cultural management did not add up to a whole. As I reviewed the field, I began to focus on strategic issues. How should firms select, develop, and manage globally competent networks of people who can implement firms' increasingly international, multinational, and global business strategies? The work I've been doing more recently, both as a researcher and a consultant, combines the international people management skills with international business strategy.

Battaglia: It is almost as if you are feeling your way in the dark, or perhaps in the twilight.

Adler: In part, yes. At the time I was getting my Ph.D. in organizational behavior and organization development from UCLA, there was no field of international organizational behavior or global organization development. I had to find people I could learn from to create my own set of learnings.

Battaglia: A number of years ago, you wrote about the corporate world becoming more interrelated and more international. Yet less then five percent of organizational behavior articles published in top American management journals have focused on cross-cultural issues. How has the focus changed in the last five years?

Adler: Unfortunately, the answer is not very positive. When I published a review article in 1983 entitled "Cross-Cultural Management: The Ostrich and the Trend," we really thought the academic world was acting like an ostrich. It was hiding from the trend of *going international* rather than choosing to see it and its importance. The survey reviewed 24 of the leading management journals in the United States; both those directed at corporate audiences such as *Harvard Business Review* and those directed at researchers such as the *Academy of Management Journal.* The results showed fewer then five percent of the articles were international or cross-cultural.

Colleagues who replicated my study in the late-1980s found exactly the same percentage of international and cross-cultural articles. Unfortunately, while I found absolutely no increasing trend from 1970 to 1980, they similarly found no trend across the 1980s. I find these results very discouraging. My own sense is that awareness of the importance of cross-cultural management has begun to change only in the last two years.

A colleague, Dr. Nakiye Boyacigiller (School of Business, San Jose State University), and I just published an article in the *Academy of Management Review*. In the article entitled "The Parochial Dinosaur: The Organizational Sciences in a Global Context," we systematically question why there are so few articles on international and cross-cultural management. You can tell from the title, our conclusion is that the shift to a more international perspective is happening very slowly.

In the article, we conclude that management is still very ethnocentric and focused primarily on the United States. Management theories incorporate primarily U.S. cultural values. For instance, motivation theories published in the United States mainly emphasize the individual; whereas in many other cultures in the world, the emphasis should be on the group. In those cultures, the individual is motivated by the benefit to the group, whether that group is the extended family or a team of colleagues at work. The importance of group versus individual motivation varies both by country and by region of the world. Predictably in the United States, which is the most individualistic country in the world, our motivation theories are based on the individual.

To use another example, there is a similar dichotomy between cultures assuming individual free will and those believing in determinism. American culture strongly believes in free will; the individual can do what he or she chooses to do. Similarly, at the country level (the collective level), Americans assume they can politically, economically, and militarily influence events in the ways we desire. Americans intervene to make things go their way.

Whereas in many other parts of the world, there are strong beliefs in determinism (in events being beyond control). In those cultures, it is not that individual action is irrelevant, but rather that determinism also plays a significant role. For instance in the Middle East, there is an Arabic saying, "En Shah Allah," which means "If God is willing." "En Shah Allah" means that if anything is going to happen, I must do my best and God must want it to happen. It will not happen just by individual action. By contrast, in the United States, you can not say to your manager, "This road will get built, "En Shah Allah." Your American boss will respond by telling you that either the road is completed by the specified deadline, or you are no longer employed.

Americans generally do not accept that there are many things beyond their control. According to Americans, removing the uncertainties and, thus, the lack of control is what good planning and good management are for—identifying and planning for the contingencies. External versus internal attribution distinguishes at the individual level between determinism and free will. The American managers generally score very high on internal attribution (e.g., free will). MBAs, as a group, score extremely high on internal attribution.

Battaglia: Can you comment on the role of organization development given the growing globalization of business and organizations?

Adler: Interestingly, internal attribution shows up prominently in the area of organization development. Organization development prides itself in being value-based, unlike most other management functions which do not define themselves in terms of values. Most organization development values are almost completely coincident with American values. For example, one of the assumptions underlying organizational change is that change is good. Not all cultures agree. American managers, based on American cultural values, generally take a problem-solving, problem-oriented, change-enhancing, the-future-can-be-made-better approach.

Some cultures in other parts of the world value the past more. They are conservative (in the literal sense, not in the political sense). They emphasize learning from the past and, in particular, learning from the wisdom of the elders. They do not emphasize change and the future to the extent that Americans do.

Similarly with regard to leadership, Americans often assume top management, often times the charismatic founder, can create a particular organizational culture. Part of that belief relates to our assumptions concerning free will versus determinism and individualism versus collectivism. American culture does not really believe in determinism. Therefore, there is an implicit assumption that employees come to the company "tabula rasa;" as a blank slate upon which the organization's culture can be written. Contrast this view with a fundamental assumption of cross-cultural management, which is that adults have certain attitudes which, based on the culture in which they grew up, are set (generally concerning what is, to them, their perceptions and thoughts about the world, and how they believe one should behave in the world).

Battaglia: I remember reading your findings that organization culture cannot necessarily change the basic culture of the individual.

Adler: True. Some extremely interesting research has been conducted on that issue. It addressed the question, "Can people be changed and, if so, how fast can they change — especially as their firms change to become more global in their organizational strategies and structures. The implicit assumption has been that people also are becoming more similar as their organizations become more similar. As companies developed global marketing strategies, they were assuming most people in the world will want similar goods and services.

Interestingly, that assumption was tested in two major research studies conducted by Europeans. Dr. Geert Hofstede, a Dutch researcher, studied IBM. He surveyed 116,000 employees and managers across 40 countries, later extending the study to 70 countries. He found that culture explained 50 percent of the differences among managers working in each of the countries at IBM. Even though IBM is seen as having one of the strongest corporate cultures in the world, national culture still impacted it and explained half the variance in managerial behavior.

During the same time period, Dr. André Laurent, a professor at INSEAD in France, surveyed managers in nine western European countries and the United States. He studied how managers differed in their day-to-day managerial behavior (e.g., would they bypass their boss to get a job done). Laurent found significant differences across the nine western European countries and the United States. He has now expanded his study to include several Asian countries. Both Hofstede's and Laurent's studies are excellent pieces of research.

Additional research by Laurent revealed some intriguing findings on the question of convergence versus divergence; whether managers are becoming more similar or maintaining their dissimilarity across countries. Laurent repeated his earlier research within a single multinational corporation. He expected that there would be some cultural differences but that they would be smaller than in the original multi-company study due to the overlay of a shared corporate culture. To his surprise, he found that the cross-national differences got bigger.

In replicating the study in a second and a third multinational company, he again found that the differences got bigger. The Germans got more German; the French got more French; the Swedes got more Swedish, and the Italians got more Italian. Experts in the field do not know exactly why the difference got bigger. Their best guess is that when you are exposed to a foreign culture, you tend to express your own culture more prominently. For instance, a German working for an American corporation is immersed in the "Americanness" of the corporate culture. To maintain his identity, he finds himself needing to express his "Germanness" more distinctly. Laurent's findings support those of Hofstede.

Battaglia: In the United States, training and organization development are taking a lead role in assisting organizations is in the areas of quality management and productivity improvement. What do you see as the most important international areas?

Adler: For American organizations and corporations, the first issue is awareness. The United States has been so economically successful for so many years that it does not occur to many managers that they need to do things differently in the future to perpetuate their past pattern of success. To continue to prosper, many firms which have their major operations in the United States must expand to include other countries. However, for many, awareness to the fact that they have to conduct business quite differently to succeed abroad is still not there. Accepting the need to change is an extremely hard lesson to learn when you have been as economically successful as the United States has been for so long.

The second major issue is education. Unfortunately, the U.S. educational system lacks an international emphasis. Students take little or no geography, and they rarely study anything outside of the United States. I know in my 12 years of education (K-12) in California, we studied California history extensively, we studied United States history, and we spent one week on world history. Organizations, however, need people who understand the rest of the world. If they do not get that background during their formal education, they must get it as adults from their corporations.

That is definitely an issue for many American managers, yet not as much of an issue for managers from other countries. Most education systems in other developed countries do teach children about both their own and other cultures. The gap between the standard education of Americans versus that of our Asian and European counterparts concerns me because I think Americans should be able to continue to successfully play a creative role in the world economy, but they will not be able to without new skills.

Battaglia: What are some of those new skills?

Adler: The first is awareness; the second, education; and the third is major organizational change. To shift from domestically-centered organizations to internationally-centered firms requires major change. All of our organization change tools need to be used to help organizations make that transition. There has been a lot of talk in the United States about wanting to have a "level playing field;" an open and fair set of economic rules for all countries' firms and markets. However, the problem with a "level playing field" is that *it is level.* What that means when you look at organization strategy, structure, and human resource systems is that Americans do not have an inherent advantage. Talent will flow to opportunity. Best firms will dominate global markets. That is a very significant change.

Battaglia: How will this effect senior executives?

Adler: If you look at the senior management of major corporations, there has definitely been a "passport" glass ceiling in the same way as there has been a glass ceiling for women or other subgroups within the United States. Generally, you cannot get into senior management in a Japanese corporation unless you are Japanese, in a U.S. corporation unless you are American, or a German corporation unless you are German.

Moreover, there are other significant trends emerging as global economic changes translate into new global strategies, and those strategies into global structure. Global firms make very different decisions from those of domestic firms on such questions as where the corporation should be headquartered, where its major operations are located, who will run each operation worldwide, what management style dominates the corporation, and which types of career paths will lead to success.

Battaglia: Are all of these things being developed, or are corporations still developing them at this time?

Adler: Some corporations are at the pre-awareness stage; some are at the awareness stage; some, at the exploratory stage; and some at the implementation stage. A few leading firms have developed very creative, impressive ways of addressing many of these issues. However, I am not aware of any firm that feels 100 percent satisfied that it knows exactly how to structure and operate a global corporation. From the human resource perspective of creating globally competent people, several European firms have gone further than most United States firms. Still there are some outstanding United States firms in terms of their creativity and the changes they are implementing.

Battaglia: What actions are international firms taking that are effective and exciting?

Adler: For most firms, their strategies are proprietary, but I can mention several examples of very creative approaches. Each example is a piece of the puzzle, rather than the whole puzzle.

Citicorp has taken a number of highly creative steps in educating and training its managers. For example, from the first year of employment, individuals who are considered "fast track" anywhere in the world are assigned to at least one project team in which the focus is global and the membership is multinational. Although all members have their regular jobs, they also have at least one situation in which they can apply their expertise to a global problem. Compare this to traditional career paths in which you only start thinking globally once you have reached senior management.

Citicorps' process develops the ability to think globally starting the first year of employment, rather than as something that gets tacked on the end of one's career. Needless to say, the multinational task force requires members to develop the process skills necessary for cooperating with people from different cultures.

Bull HN, which is the merger between American Honeywell and France's Groupe Bull, developed an executive training program that took 25 of its senior executives to five countries to meet with leaders from all sectors — corporate, political, technological, the media, etc. Because the executives were involved in formulating a global strategy, the executive program became equally global with multinational participants, multinational presenters, multinational venues, and multinational issues. Bull HN's executives devoted five weeks to the process; definitely a significant commitment of time.

For many years, AT&T had the luxury of being a domestic monopoly in terms of its domination of its home industry. When the rules changed in the 1980s, AT&T found itself competing against some of the most significant players in the telecommunications industry world. Realizing that some of their senior executives lacked broad international experience, the company had each of its top 100 senior executives "adopt" a country.

Adopting a country meant visiting the country; getting to know the country and the operations there in depth; and staying current on economic, political, and cultural developments in the country. The result was that when the senior executives met, they brought a high level of country-specific expertise to the situation being discussed. Adopting a country was an excellent way to both educate the individuals and to bring global expertise to corporate decision making. Certainly, it would have been nice if each of the executives had received the same kind of expertise in school, but they had not, so the corporation created a way to bridge the gap.

Battaglia: What you have described is almost like group learning, only at the global and international level.

Adler: Exactly. Another example is Arthur Andersen and Company. Arthur Andersen is structured somewhat differently than a corporation because it is a partnership. A board of partners comprised of 24 people serves as the senior governing board. Until recently, only about six partners were non-American, and of those six, most were from Anglo cultures—Canada, Britain, Australia—cultures similar to the United States.

As of this past year when Larry Weinbach became Chief Executive Partner, 50 percent of the partners on the governing board are non-American. Based on this fundamental change, the most senior decisions are now made by partners who bring to each discussion a worldwide perspective. This change enables the firm to "think globally, while acting locally."

Battaglia: What else should individuals and organizations do to be better prepared to operate in a global environment?

Adler: Individuals need to be extremely customer sensitive so that, even while working globally, they can identify small niche markets and tailor products or services to a particular clientele.

Organizations need to attract the best and brightest people worldwide. However, the best and the brightest do not all live in a single country. They must recruit worldwide. Similarly, good people must be promoted without regard to nationality. If there is a "passport" ceiling, the corporation will not retain its best people. A company may deny that there is a "passport" ceiling, but its existence becomes evident when one reviews the executive suite and notices that only executives from certain countries are in senior management or in the queue to become senior managers.

Battaglia: Then the brightest and most talented people today look to see if upper management includes people from many cultures?

Adler: Absolutely. But if we reexamine the expatriate issue, an unfortunate pattern occurred. In the past, organizations did not consider international experience to be very important. They assumed that all of the most important things were happening at home. They tended to send their good, but not great, employees abroad. At times, companies were lucky and attracted very good employees for international assignments because the people chose to take the foreign position for personal rather than professional reasons. When those employees returned after their foreign stay, they had been forgotten: "Out of sight, out of mind." On average, going abroad hurt people's careers. Now companies face a dilemma in trying to attract more people—and, in particular, in trying to attract their best and brightest to go abroad. These employees, knowing how former expatriates were treated, respond with, "Excuse me, I do not want to go abroad if it is going to hurt my career." The companies say, "Oh no, that won't happen to you." But the best employees are skeptical and may refuse to go abroad.

Battaglia: Can you comment on the role of organization development given the growing globalization of business and organizations?

Adler: To the extent that a massive shift is occurring, there is definitely a critical role for organization development. My caveat, though, is that that does not mean making the rest of the world like the United States. The field of organization development has to look inward and ask several questions: What are our values? To what extent are those American values defined as organization development values? To what extent do we need to change our values, our processes, our perspective, our ways of doing things, and our profession to be most helpful to a global organization?

In my mind, the core of organization development is critically necessary. However, some of its forms must change. The skills and approaches that have been most valuable in the 1960s and 1970s for American organizations or organizations dominantly operating in the United States may not be the most appropriate, valuable, or effective ones for global corporations.

Battaglia: In your international consulting experience, what organization development skills have you found to be helpful or transferable?

Adler: Of all your questions, that is the hardest so far. One of the core issues that organization development focuses on is change and resistance to change. So distinguishing between resistance to change and people not liking "X" is a helpful notion, especially when the changes are extensive. When everything is changing—language, culture, business protocol—the concept of resistance to change aids in managing the process of change rather than just managing the specific content of the organizational transformation.

Secondly, organization development views shared vision as a uniting force. With an international or multinational company, the process for creating shared vision changes somewhat because people contribute in different ways to thinking about and talking about a vision. But creating that vision or re-creating one is extremely important. The vision needs to be inclusive of people from all parts of the world within the organization's domain, rather than just from the headquarter's culture or from one particular country. That is just as true for a German firm needing to look outside of Germany as it is for an American firm looking to Europe.

For example, this past year, Siemens AG, a major German corporation, prepared a film for its senior executives. Siemens' executives from around the world described how Siemens' German culture helps them conduct business globally, how it hinders their global success, and how the firm needs to change to continue its success into the next century.

Battaglia: So, they really made a major effort to globalize the thinking of their people.

Adler: Yes. In addition, Siemens, Fiat, and many other European-based companies are requiring their managers to be bilingual. In the majority of cases, these European managers are multilingual, speaking three, four, and five languages fluently.

Battaglia: Is English becoming the business language in the world?

Adler: Yes, English has become the most common business language. However, I strongly believe that the most effective global managers are at least bilingual. When you are bilingual, you see the world differently. You are able to hold multiple perspectives more easily, and you are able to sympathize and communicate more easily with people who are working in a non-native language.

Battaglia: People think of language as just words, but it is more. It is the understanding and comprehension that relates to the words.

Adler: Absolutely. In some sense, it does not make such a difference if you know all the specific languages of the people with whom you are working. Oftentimes, there are four, five, or six different native languages at the table. However, the fact that you can speak in at least one other language is important.

Battaglia: Are there any other skills that are transferable and necessary?

Adler: Yes. Important skills include tolerance for ambiguity, stress management, and relationship building. Consider relationship building. Almost every culture (other than American culture) first questions who you are and then decides if they want to do business with you. Whereas in the United States, Americans first ask the task question, "Can we do business together?" If the business goes well, Americans then might want to develop a relationship with the other person.

Battaglia: In relation to your Cultural Synergy Model of management, have you found international organizations that successfully depict this model? If so, who and how?

Adler: Different organizations use cultural synergy in different ways. The basic notion of cultural synergy is to recognize cultural differences, value them, and use them to benefit the organization. Today, more organizations are considering cultural differences as a resource rather than as a problem or something to be ignored.

Not surprisingly, the model can be applied to domestic cultural diversity issues as well as to international issues. I mentioned earlier the film that Siemens produced to examine its global role. The film followed the Cultural Synergy Model, focusing first on recognizing the differences and then on how to use them to benefit Siemens business culture.

One of the phrases being used more for domestic workforce 2000 issues is valuing diversity. Synergy goes beyond valuing differences. It is not just recognizing you as different and valuing that difference. That is step one of cultural synergy. The next step is to ask how I can combine your difference with my difference to create an organization that is stronger, more effective, and more successful than it is without those differences.

Cultural synergy is not a multi-domestic model. It requires more than merely having a bunch of different cultures or countries represented. It goes beyond valuing diversity to ask, "How can we use the differences to the benefit of the organization?"

Battaglia: Thank you for a very informative and thought-provoking interview. You have given organization development consultants food for thought. As our clients turn to globalization, it behooves us to look at globalizing our own skills, techniques, and interventions.

References

Adler, Nancy J. "Reentry: Managing Cross-Cultural Transitions." *Group and Organization Studies,* 6 no. 3 (1981): pp. 341-356.

Adler, Nancy J. "A Portable Life," (videotape) documents the role of the spouse in international transfers.

Adler, Nancy J. "Cross-Cultural Management: The Ostrich and the Trend." *Academy of Management Review,* 8 nos. 1-2 (1983): pp. 7-45.

Adler, Nancy J. Chapter 4 of *International Dimensions of Organizational Behavior.* Boston: PWS Kent, 1991 (for Cultural Synergy Model).

Adler, Nancy J. Chapters 8 and 9 of *International Dimensions of Organizational Behavior,* 2d ed. PWS—Kent Publishing, 1991 (for a discussion of expatriate issues from the perspective of the employee and the spouse).

Adler, Nancy J. and Ghadar, Fariborz. "Strategic Human Resource Management: A Global Perspective." In *Human Resource Management In International Comparison,* edited by Rudiger Pieper. Berlin: deGruyter, 1990: pp. 235-260.

Adler, Nancy J. and Jelinek, Mariann. "Is 'Organization Culture' Culture Bound?" *Human Resource Management,* 25 no.1 (1986): pp. 73-80.

Boyacigiller, Nakiye and Adler, Nancy J. "The Parochial Dinosaur: The Organizational Sciences in a Global Context." *Academy of Management Review,* 16 no. 2 (1991): pp. 262-290.

12. TQM: OD's Role in Implementing Value-Based Strategies

Melville Adams

Traditional organizational development as a change methodology emphasizing action research, openness, and internal commitment has been pointing in the right direction, and many firms have benefited from such interventions. But changing times and world economic realities now demand organizational change based on new strategies and change methodologies.

The latest paradigm shift integrates concepts and tools from strategic management and quality management to refocus organizations on creating and improving customer value. This chapter discusses why OD efforts now frequently fall short, and suggests ways in which OD can play a role in implementing the new paradigm.

Introduction

Foreign competitors have achieved substantial market share by providing better value to customers. Apologists for U.S. firms often cite cheaper financing and synergistic cultural values as the bases for this success, but many American consumers simply perceive that foreign firms provide better quality. The Japanese, sensitive to blame for any decline in the U.S. economy, attribute their quality and share gains to better management. They rub salt in this wound, ironically, by crediting Americans Sarasohn, Protzman (Forbes, 1989), and W. Edwards Deming (Walton, 1986) for teaching them an approach to management based on continuous improvement of systems through statistical process control (SPC) techniques.

Acceptance of Deming's ideas by U.S. managers has been underwhelming with adoption coming only as a last resort by firms with shrinking market share. As a statistician, Deming advised on management theory and style from outside the field. He chastised leadership, criticized motivation schemes, and ridiculed managers for rewarding and punishing individual performances that are due mostly to random variation. His abrasive style, lack of grounding in management theory, and ambiguous implementation turned off many managers and academics on first hearing.

Many managers and employees perceive quality management as just the latest quick fix commanded by top management. SPC, TQM (Total Quality Management), and QFD (Quality Function Deployment) are often assumed to be just the latest top management fads with the same short expected life spans of other three letter programs. But these "cures" originated with

Melville Adams is Assistant Professor of Management at the University of Alabama in Huntsville, Huntsville, AL 35899.

industrial engineers rather than business schools. Most management experts, including OD consultants, did not understand the underlying philosophy, comprehensiveness of the systematic methodology, and the unique benefits to be gained, so they offered little encouragement. Even with top management commitment, many programs failed as managers could not overcome structural barriers to implementation. Thus, after flirting with quality circles (in which managers often blamed employees for poor results), U.S. managers' initial interest in approaches based on quality languished in the late 1970s.

Likewise, academics in organizational development (OD) and strategic management, upon hearing bits of Deming's approach that sound familiar, often conclude that statistically-based quality management is merely traditional organizational development in disguise. To these experts, almost any OD program will achieve some improvement, and there is nothing so unique in quality management based on process control as to require its use. Yet, in spite of nearly continuous OD programs on team building, job redesign or enrichment, revised reward systems, and multiple reorganizations, many domestic firms lost their competitive advantage and customer loyalty.

Given the Japanese example and obvious market signals, these managers and academics should reconsider. The ongoing erosion of market shares, constant improvement in quality by Japanese producers, even the redefinition of quality (Woodruff, 1990) have made many managers look beyond quality circles to the basic philosophy inherent in quality management. The adoption of just-in-time (JIT) inventory systems provided a major impetus to quality management since JIT succeeds only if incoming materials meet quality requirements. Likewise, concurrent engineering depends on typical quality-based strategies including systems integration across functions and intense focus on the customer (Evans, 1988; Ziemke & McCollum, 1990).

Many managers have attempted to use these approaches in a piecemeal fashion and failed, even with the help of OD consultants. Cultural differences, short-term financial orientations, and labor restrictions each attract blame. However, some managers achieve quantum leaps without OD specialists by understanding the integrated systems philosophy underlying TQM, SPC, and QFD.

Recently, strategic management researchers generalized and extended these quality-based approaches into a modified strategic management paradigm designated "value-based management" (Carothers & Adams, 1990). Value-based management prescribes a top management predisposition to provide the best net value to the customer by designing and continuously improving systems to create and deliver that value. This chapter outlines key differences in results between the traditional paradigm and value-based management, defines the basic requirements for value-based management and suggests some roles that OD can play in implementing this new paradigm.

Does Quality Matter?

Even in favorable environments, firms that are apparently well-managed (i.e., they do many of the right things well) often fail to achieve superior results. Using good selection criteria and procedures, they hire good people, train them to do the tasks required for their job, and provide financial incentives for above average performance. Strategic planners often set clear performance objectives, usually for sales growth and profitability, then raise and allocate the required resources. Many even adopt a soft form of quality management by adding a broad quality goal, quality slogans, and training in team building.

The usual result of such well-intended but incomplete efforts is mediocre performance as measured by both customer and investor. Motorola, Inc. benchmarked quality using the concept of standard deviations from the mean (sigma) of the distribution of process outcomes. It found that typical well-managed firms and processes operated at about ±4 sigma but that best-in-class firms achieve ±6 sigma with very few in between (Therrien, 1989; Gill, 1990; Wiggenhorn, 1990; Smith, 1989).

If a process has 1,200 steps (or a product has 1,200 parts) and the mean shifts up or down as much as 1.5 sigma, the cumulative effect of 4 sigma quality is to send customers a product that averages 3.24 defects per unit! Only 4 percent of the output would be defect-free. It is no wonder that U.S. car makers have consistently shipped cars averaging 10-30 defects and airlines lose luggage. However, 6 sigma quality will send no more than 3.4 defects per million units (99.6-99.9999998 percent perfect). This level of quality truly approaches zero defects and is well on the way to providing total customer satisfaction.

Higher quality improves financial performance (Capon, Farley, & Hoenig, 1990) as does customer orientation (Narver and Slater, 1990). At 4 sigma, a firm will spend at least 10 percent of sales on scrap, rework, and repair; a 6 sigma firm will spend less than 1 percent. This quantifies what both Deming and Crosby have preached for years; that quality management usually lowers total cost. Thus, the average (4 sigma) firm cannot compete with a 6 sigma firm for long. The question is: What is the difference in management between merely good and world-class firms?

There appears to be at least four additional factors at work in achieving extremely high levels of quality. First, top management adopts a strategic intent to be the best and to continuously improve the firm's ability to satisfy customers' needs. Second, top management adopts and inculcates in employees an integrated, cross-functional process orientation. Third, to manage the improvement effort, top management adopts a quantified set of quality objectives and measures based on process variability. Finally, managers consistently manage to those objectives by defining, implementing, and controlling key cross-functional operating plans to reach them.

One key to implementation is SPC, since it provides the substance to the intent. Why is SPC required? Most importantly, it drives systems definition and process thinking more thoroughly than other approaches. The use of process flow charts and cause-effect diagrams quickly illuminates the cross-functional nature of organizational problems.

Given the intent to be world-class, SPC also provides the only technology to *systematically* define, control, and reduce variation and increase customer value across all systems. Intent without a statistically quantified, systems approach remains only wishful thinking. Likewise, SPC without intent quickly becomes a quick fix. Employees in either situation soon realize management is paying only lip service.

Further, grounding management decisions in the quantitative language of variation removes the inherent subjectivity of qualitative judgments in decision making and performance evaluations. Managers and employees alike are forced to understand the process in its entirety, the causes of variation, and the relationship between the capability of the process and the customers' requirements. The objectivity of SPC forces management to admit that 95 percent of the problems are management's responsibility and to quit worrying about the 5 percent that can be blamed on employees.

Another important reason has to do with employee relations and management style. The additional information empowers employees to take control of the process and make suggestions for improvement. This alone can change the traditionally adversarial relationship with management into a cooperative one.

Finally, rather than each sub-unit solving its own problems and sub-optimizing system and firm performance, SPC keeps improvement efforts focused on the end-user, even if a given employee has only internal "customers." Changes must increase customer value. Obviously, integrated and sustained management of systems changes an SPC effort into value-based management. What are the essential ingredients of value-based management?

Basic Requirements for Value-Based Management

Rather than delegating quality, the CEO and other senior executives must learn to become managerial leaders rather than administrators (Kotter, 1990; Bounds & Dobbins, 1991). Top management must take both strategic and operational actions to continuously improve customer value.

Top Management Strategic Initiatives

The strategic initiatives top management must take roughly follow the strategic management process models but are modified by customer orientation. First, to motivate employees and focus resources, senior managers must define the mission and strategic intent. Rather than a product focus, the mission must take responsibility for satisfying some fundamental customer need with the best net value. Strategic intent establishes a sustained, long-term effort to achieve global leadership in the mission (Hamel & Prahalad, 1989).

Second, in operationalizing this vision, the CEO must set ambitious quantified objectives and define a common metric for measuring progress toward the objectives. With customer satisfaction paramount, quality objectives rank before any other objectives, but broad profit goals should be included. Then all managers must manage to quality targets more intensively than to traditional objectives, especially financial ones. To achieve unity, management must focus on one or two key measures of quality or cycle time that are stated in statistical terms so they apply to all sub-units.

Third, top management must define a long-term strategic plan and annual operational initiatives designed to reach the objectives. Although quality, cost, and schedule are inseparable, the long-term plan must be driven by a generic strategy of quality differentiation, not low cost, and a grand strategy consistent with value improvement. Cooperative strategies may be more productive than competitive market penetration and market development. Focused strategies build on quality initiatives more than diversification.

Fourth, managers must obtain support through an iterative, participative planning process, goal directed incentives for managers and employees, and coordinated training in why and how at all levels. In most firms, this will require changes in culture, management style, and human resource management practices. Structural changes may be required but must not segregate quality into its own box. Integration is also enhanced by identical rate of improvement goals for all areas.

Fifth, to get results, top management must review results using the common statistical metric and objectives, even when the environment has provided an excuse to forget the long-term plan. A performance measurement system must be established and publicized, then used frequently by senior management in reviewing operations. These reviews will fail unless quality and system improvement lead the agenda. Motorola looks at defects per unit or process step, final quality audit results, out-of-box quality delivered to the customer, product warranty, and cost of quality.

Sixth, management must reward results. Due to the need to change culture, intrinsic motivation is almost certainly more important than extrinsic. What is needed is group celebration of group improvements, not personal reward of individual achievements. Formal quality awards from the CEO's office, public recognition of recipients and the reason for their award provide symbols beyond those in the daily contact with employees. Extrinsic, financial gains can be shared with those who contributed, but only if this is pay for normal job performance—not one time successes.

Finally, managers must modify the process as necessary to sustain their strategic intent. Almost always, implementation will be more difficult than strategy formulation, primarily because invalid assumptions were made. Top management must be willing to increase investment to overcome barriers but unwilling to scale back the objectives. In short, managers must redefine their role toward leadership and take responsibility for system ownership.

Operational Initiatives

Beyond these strategic roles, management must also lay out an implementation plan to reach what usually appears to be an impossible quality improvement target. While this sounds like a very mechanistic model, the actual implementation requires a very organic approach. Considerable interpretation is required to define what the overall plan means to sub-units. This depends on participative management, employee involvement, and cross-functional integration. First, each employee must understand that the basic improvement process includes at least five steps.

- Identify customers and what they value at all levels. Senior managers must regularly visit key current and potential customers to determine what they like and do not like. Functional managers and employees must not only know what the firm's customers value, they must also know who they serve internally and what these internal customers value.

- Identify product/service provided. In determining customer value, managers and employees must focus on which product or service they provide that is valued by the customer. Customers have begun to value service as highly as product quality. Better service results from reducing cycle times.

- Define processes. The actual process used by employees in both manufacturing and service units is usually not the designed process, the process understood by management, or the process that produces best value. Improvement is possible only by understanding each actual system in its entirety. Thus, cross-functional teams must flow chart existing processes, including all steps, inventory, and feedback loops. All personnel impacted by the process should agree that the flow chart accurately describes the process as they interact with it.

- Simplify the process. Eliminate mistakes and unnecessary steps. Define quality in from the beginning with concurrent engineering. Eliminate inventory. Maximize real-time feedback by giving employees first opportunity to correct process inefficiencies and errors.

- Continuously improve. Measure, analyze, and control the process through SPC. Initial improvement results from reducing variability (i.e., making the process more capable of meeting engineering specs). The most important improvement, though, comes from moving the average in the direction that increases value to the customer.

A second set of operational initiatives concerns integrating mechanisms and management style. The firm must define the cross-functional systems that impact customer value and integrate management efforts across these functions. Top management must drive participative management throughout the organization and gain cooperation between sub-units. These initiatives include team building, establishing ownership, and changing the culture. These are discussed more fully by looking at the role of organization development in achieving superior results.

How is Value-Based Strategic Change Different From OD?

Traditional OD and value-based management share several concepts and principles; so many that OD specialists often view TQM as a special case of OD. However, since each uses key concepts such as system, quality, and change somewhat differently, any role for OD in implementing value-based management requires some modification of the traditional OD approaches.

Systems

Both models hold an open systems view of organizations in which environmental forces exert pressure for certain outcomes. Value-based management defines both external and internal systems from the customer's point of view, and includes after-sale attributes that impact net value. Rather than functional, value-*adding* systems, these value-*contributing* systems are defined *across* functions to focus on those activities that impact customers' valued attributes such as quality, reliability, longevity, availability, serviceability, affordability, image, etc. Obviously, the determination of the customer's value criteria is critical.

For example, nearly all car owners place a high value on reliability. Along with manufacturing, the cross-functional system for reliability includes marketing, customer service, dealers, records, parts supply, etc. Many American manufacturers translated this into warranty programs to provide "free" fixes for any problem in a specified period. This strategy only irritated customers who were required to spend more time and effort to document ownership, maintain their vehicle's maintenance and repair history, and make repeated trips to dealers. In effect, auto makers held customers responsible for quality. This switch happened in spite of an open systems view, because that view was still focused on short-term financial performance.

In value-based management, the open systems view requires top management to take responsibility for providing what the customer values in all functions and departments. This cross-functional approach begins with the design process and strategic planning, includes all staff functions, and concludes with anyone dealing with customers after the sale or service contact to determine the role each plays in the system for providing value. For example, each function is scrutinized for its impact on reliability. Thus, system definition is based on relevant customer values, not just engineering or management notions of key functions.

Quality

Many OD projects have emphasized quality ever since the end of WWII, but the notion of quality has been redefined by the SPC approach. Rather than the usual approach in which OD consultants let clients define what quality means, value-based management requires managers and employees to take responsibility for determining what the customer values. Then managers must agree on how this value is best defined and measured in statistical terms.

Traditional OD approaches may assume that adaptive change within a function is good and, thus, end with simple outcome measures of quality defined internally by marketing, production, or engineering. These measures rely on either technically derived definitions of quality related to engineering specifications or more qualitative measures. Even though specs include tolerances, neither approach *controls* random variation inherent in every process, and both lose sight of attributes valued by the customer. Such measures promote the use of cost/benefit analyses which result in acceptance and delivery of "tolerable" (i.e., minimum required quality). Unfortunately, cost analyses never measure the cost of poor quality in the loss of potential customers ("unknown and unknowable," Deming, 1985) and only measure losses of current customers after the fact, when market shares are reported.

In statistically-based approaches, attributes valued by the customer define quality. Further, these definitions are operationalized by statistical variances in the output at each step in the process. Only when variation in output is in control *AND* within engineering specifications can the firm claim that it is delivering the desired quality. Merely meeting specifications may still yield inconsistent quality and no information on how to improve the process.

Many managers believe value-based management and its cousins TQM or SPC do not apply to service organizations. In fact, service functions often provide the best opportunities to improve customer value, but quality measures usually differ from those in manufacturing. Since service almost always has a time component, goals often focus on improving the *rate* at which service is provided or reducing the *frequency* of errors, given a system in control.

Organization Change

The traditional OD approach to organizational consultation assumes that organizations must frequently (if not continuously) adapt, face up to problems, and change, but that individuals too frequently do not like to change because they perceive that change will affect them adversely. Managers often try to make changes (the "logical" part of the process) without regard for the readiness of people to accept and support those changes. Indeed, without their full support, employees can torpedo a plan or even make a brilliant plan look stupid.

People are confronted with hundreds of demands, large and small, every day. They can't respond to them all. Thus, the OD consultant must be an expert on helping organizations marshall employees and other stakeholders for identifying and making necessary changes.

Kurt Lewin's famous "unfreeze-change-refreeze" model suggests periods of stability surrounding each change event. This implies that the intent of an intervention is to fix a problem. Resulting improvement may be sporadic, problem-oriented, and crisis driven. Unfreezing a system helps break through inertia by getting those involved to see the need for change. But value-based management suggests that organizations must get beyond participants' myopic internal views. Without a focus on improving customer value, unfreezing a system will likely increase variation in individual and system performance. Further, while Lewin's model assumes that unfreezing can be started at any point in the organization, value-based management insists that the required link to the organization's mission and strategic intent can be made only if the unfreezing and change effort is led by top management.

Deming refuses to consult without starting at the top. Motorola executives give a senior manager credit for calling attention to low quality and starting the unfreezing process for top management. It is doubtful that a bottom-up approach to OD can initiate a 6 sigma level of quality. However, OD can play a critical role in extending the unfreezing beyond top management by communicating the need for change throughout the organization.

After individuals and/or groups are unfrozen, the NIH (Not Invented Here) syndrome often arises. OD seized early on the benefits of giving employees a problem to solve, pointing out that poor solutions cannot be accepted if better solutions are available, and then helping them search for the best alternative. Value management reduces the tendency for NIH, not by giving the problem to the employees but by making both employees and managers more responsive to the customer's problem.

OD also recognized that reasonable effort to plan, followed by action, and then research to fine tune is necessary. So life must include constant action-research on all key issues, though the cycle time varies with the issue. This philosophy has been applied to "formal" research such as production, outputs, employee attitudes, and turnover as well as more informal research such as perceptions of progress against stated goals. This is all well and good if the problem is at the employee level. If not (as is the case with 95 percent of the variation), then OD's role is limited unless it teaches cross-functional systems management with top management involvement.

The third step is refreezing the change into common everyday practice, until it is replaced by another cycle of action research. Like value-based management, OD requires some sort of monitoring system, formal written reports and pre-arranged checkup meetings, or informal instantaneous feedback on agreed-upon issues. OD supports such informal processes with extensive norm-building within the group to see that this freezing actually happens, rather than simply being an ideal plan on a forgotten memo. But value-based management assumes that improvement is continuously possible, and that only the process of continuous improvement should be "refrozen." Thus, managers must anticipate what customers will value next.

In addition to understanding how the environment will impact customers' perceived value, the firm can look to environmental changes, particularly in the technological and social arenas, for new ways to improve its capability to provide best value. OD plays a key role in value-based management by facilitating the cultural change that must take place to turn managers into customer-driven leaders of system improvement and employees into collaborative, customer-driven process improvers. Thus, OD is a non-prescriptive methodology and process for problem solution and change, whereas customer value approaches are a prescriptive, fundamental management philosophy.

OD's Role in Implementing Value-Based Management

People and norms are unfrozen, changed, and refrozen through activities called "interventions." A key to intervention success is in hooking each individual's interests, benefits, and beliefs about success (i.e., "owning"). This is often accomplished by having people experience little successes with their own real issues, then building on these to get to even more fundamental issues. Value-based management experience has shown that this process is most successful when ownership is established at the top first, and problems are also critical to the organization—not just individuals.

Lewin also contributed the simple concept of force fields in designing interventions. A force field recognizes pro-change forces on one side (including management's logical explanation of the situation, its legitimate power, and contingent rewards and punishments) and resistance to change on the other (including actual and imagined costs of compliance and loss of power). Lewin noted that managers usually try to force people to change by building up the forces for change, while those most affected usually resist even more as the ante is raised.

To remedy this, Lewin suggests one might achieve change more readily by also dealing with the resistances rather than simply trying to overpower them. This brings about commitment to a course of action rather than just compliance. This is why there is so much emphasis on participation in OD and TQM. People usually support decisions they participate in making more than those imposed on them. Fortunately, most people can learn to share power and influence as long as they have a lot of say in matters most critical to them personally. This has led to increased emphasis on pushing decisions down to those closest to the situation.

OD also stresses that "facts are friendly." It is better to be honest with one another and able to fix the problem than to be political and fix only the blame. It takes a lot of work to develop this kind of trust. Many interventions have little impact on this. SPC and fishbone charts help cure this by building the required base of objective, irrefutable, fair data and pointing out that top management must be willing to act on that information.

Finally, OD consulting places a lot of emphasis on defining who the client is. The client is not just the person who calls you in, or the one who pays the bill. The "client" includes those most strongly affected by the issues and who are being asked to carry out interventions. Practically, this often means dealing with no more than two or three levels in an organization with intensive consultation, while including others through data collection, etc., eventually cascading down to them more active involvement. Thus, OD has long recognized stakeholders outside of the organization as major players in goal accomplishment, so interventions often cross boundaries between an organization and its customers, suppliers, or other constituents.

OD's strength has always been cutting across sets of concerns to include political, human resource, marketing, production, finance, or other forces the clients identify as critical. An OD consultant strives to focus client attention on all of these important issues (sometimes via outside experts) using an open systems model. In that sense, OD complements value/quality management by dealing with the need for a specific change, while teaching clients how to build skills, norms, and values to help them deal with future changes. Most interventions are designed to train more than simply solve one problem. The consultant, having helped install an ability to bring about adaptive changes, then moves on while the client lives the lessons they have mastered. The intervention is complete, but the process is left behind in the client. This is known proudly as "working yourself out of a job."

What Must OD Avoid?

OD teaches clients a problem-solving method, but it is one that is unique to each situation. Value management suggests a common methodology based on statistics; only the content varies with each situation. This distinction has implications for problem definition and responsibility for solution.

Guarding Against Tampering

In OD, employees with a consultant's help can discover and fix systemic problems without using any particular methodology. Value-based management assumes that every system has natural variation that must be defined before attempting change. If this variation is beyond normal chance, the system is said to be out of control, meaning that factors other than chance (special causes) are influencing system performance. Improvements must begin with removing these special causes to achieve normal (i.e., random) variation in performance. Only then can managers attempt true system improvement in terms of first reducing variation in performance and, second, changing the mean system performance.

OD techniques may assume that organizational problems are due to special causes and that none of the problems are due to normal variation. If the problem is due to a special cause, OD specialists may happen to focus on the right one. But without process definition and statistical diagnosis of system performance, well-intentioned OD approaches may cause more problems than they cure. OD specialists may initiate a solution which is itself a special cause of variation, induce more variation, and drive the process further out of control. This is one form of what Deming aptly calls "tampering" with the system.

In both manufacturing and service, nearly all suggestions that depend on human senses to detect and correct random variation will worsen variation. Managers often tamper with individual factors (e.g., reward systems, job design, and job enrichment) in a futile attempt to improve system performance when performance problems are actually due to managerial factors (e.g., poor communication, faulty design, inadequate maintenance, or poor inputs).

A second, less common (but equally naive) assumption is that a problem is due to random variation (common causes) when special causes are actually at work (management's responsibility). In this instance, OD approaches may falsely assume the system needs "fixing" or improvement when, in fact, it is in control (i.e., the variation in performance is within the range expected by chance). Without understanding this natural variation, the OD specialist may again suggest changes which backfire; another form of tampering. Only value-based management through SPC provides systematic approaches to listing all possible causes, distinguishing in-control from out-of-control situations and isolating those causes most important to improving the capability to deliver value to customers.

Both OD and quality specialists assist the client in defining the point of attack. Specific OD tools such as group discussions and individual interviews to define and isolate key issues are also important tools of quality management. These have the specific initial goal of building a cause-effect diagram (fishbone chart) and later (with process in control), designing experiments to determine sensitivities to common causes of random variation. The objectivity and impersonality of fishbone charts, statistical measures of system performance, and experimental design ensure thorough, impartial analysis and diagnosis. Without these, other complementary tools such as quality circles often fail after quick early gains.

Authority and Responsibility

To implement these methods, both OD and value management require employees to be empowered with the authority and responsibility to make changes. But without statistical process definition and analysis, OD may hold lower levels responsible for management's problems. Although continuous improvement programs rely on employees at all levels to call attention to problems—even giving low level employees the authority to stop production lines as necessary—this is only to call attention to a management responsibility to fix the system. This individual responsibility provides the key mechanism for solving problems in real time before their cost is multiplied in successive stages of the system.

Summary

Traditionally OD assumes that organizations frequently (if not continuously) need to adapt, face up to problems and change, but that individuals (who contribute problem recognition, data, or other efforts) usually do not like to change because they perceive it will affect them adversely. Thus, the OD consultant must be an expert on helping organizations marshall the input and effort of employees and other stakeholders for identifying and making necessary changes.

OD is a generalized, non-prescriptive model for organizational change, whereas value-based management is a generalizable, prescriptive model for organizational improvement. OD leaves the selection of frameworks, problem definition, methodology, solution, and implementation up to the client/participants. Value-based management requires a superordinate framework centered on the customer, system definition, and improvement through both TQM and SPC. Value-based management will require changes similar to those of OD, and the general OD model can be very useful in implementing value-based management. But reliance on OD will not have the same results as adoption of the more specific and prescriptive value-based management model. Much OD work would be more effective if focused on systems impacting customer value.

Value-based management is at heart a management philosophy, not a technique or methodology. Nevertheless, OD specialists should be able to help overcome the extremely difficult task of implementing value-based management. OD techniques could often be used to help shorten the average 18-36 month installation process. Interviews, surveys, team building, and training are all useful mechanisms in helping managers and employees adopt a strategic intent, learn SPC, chart processes, integrate across functions, continuously improve, and change the culture to deliver better value to customers.

References

Beutow, R. Speech presented at 44th Midwest Quality Conference, Ft. Collins, CO, Oct. 4, Motorola Corp., Schaumberg, IL, 1989.

Bounds, G.M. and Dobbins, G.H. "The Manager's Job: A Paradigm Shift to a New Agenda." In M. Stahl and G. Bounds (eds.), *Competing Globally Through Customer Value: The Management of Strategic Suprasystems.* Westport, CT: Quorum Books, 1991. pp. 117-145.

Woodruff, D. "A New Era for Auto Quality." *Business Week,* (Oct. 22, 1990): pp. 84-96.

Carothers, H. and Adams, M. "Competitive Advantage Through Customer Value: The Role of Value-based Strategies." In M. Stahl and G. Bounds (eds.), *Competing Globally Through Customer Value: The Management of Strategic Suprasystems.* Westport, CT: Quorum Books, 1991. pp. 32-66.

Deming, W.E. *Out of the Crisis.* Boston: MIT and Cambridge Press, 1985.

Evans, B. "Simultaneous Engineering." *Mechanical Engineering* (February 1988): pp. 38-39.

Gill, M.S. "Stalking Six Sigma." *Business Month,* (January 1990).

Hamel, G. and Prahalad, C.K. "Strategic Intent." *Harvard Business Review,* (May-June 1989): pp. 63-76.

Hayes, R. H. "Why Japanese Factories Work." *Harvard Business Review,* (July-August 1989): pp. 56-66.

Kotter, J. P. *A Force for Change: How Leadership Differs From Management.* New York: Free Press, 1990.

Narver, J.C. and Slater, S.F. "The Effect of Market Orientation on Business Profitability." *Journal of Marketing,* 54 no. 4, (1990): pp. 20-35.

Smith, B. *The Motorola Story.* Motorola Corp., Schaumberg, IL, 1989.

Therrien, L. "The Rival Japan Respects." *Business Week* (November 13, 1989): pp. 108-114.

Walton, M. *The Deming Management Method.* New York: Putnam Publishing, 1986.

Wiggenhorn, W. "Motorola U: When Training Becomes an Education." *Harvard Business Review,* (July-August, 1990): pp. 71-83.

Wood, R. C. "A Lesson Learned and a Lesson Forgotten." *Forbes,* (Feb. 6, 1989): pp. 70-78.

Ziemke, M.C. and McCollum, J.K. "Simultaneous Engineering: Innovation or Resurrection?" *Business Forum,* 15 no. 1, (1990): pp. 14-17.